Make a
DIFFERENCE!
Be a Teacher

Compiled by
Clancy P. Hayes

Gospel Publishing House
Springfield, Missouri
02-2005

ISBN 0-88243-437-3

Contents

Preface

Make A Difference! Be A Teacher is intended to be a companion volume to *Give Them What They Want: Turning Sunday School Into A Place Where People Want To Be.* These two volumes, together with a third that is currently being developed, are meant to help teachers revitalize the ministry of Sunday School and to see their efforts become more instrumental in the transformation of their students by the Holy Spirit and the Word of God.

It is the premise of this book that teachers—through their ministry in the local church—play a vital role in the kingdom of God. Without teachers, the job of discipleship could not be done effectively. Without teachers carrying out their task, the Church would eventually die out. But we know this won't happen; Jesus assured us that the Church would never be destroyed. He keeps that promise today by continually calling men, women, boys, and girls into the spiritual role of teacher.

But some teachers feel unprepared for the task. They find themselves standing before a class each week wondering why they are there, wondering what their efforts are accomplishing for God. Because of this frustration, some abandon their calling. This need not be the case.

As you read this book, the authors hope you will find encouragement and direction for your teaching. Each of them wishes to give you a helping hand along the sometimes-rocky road of teaching. The enemy would like to trip you up, to discourage you. Use the words of this book to combat such fear and discouragement; keep fighting the good fight, especially in times of adversity.

In the first section of this volume, we go over the importance of your calling and the anointing that accompanies it. We want you to understand the significance of your influence on the lives of your students and recognize ways to strengthen that influence. We will explore the influence your example can have as well as the importance of knowing your students.

In the second section, we point out the importance of setting goals and priorities. We also explore ways to bring creativity into the classroom. Chapter seven discusses a feature of teaching that is often overlooked—connecting beliefs to behaviors. Finally, we highlight the important role teachers play in the evangelism process.

We realize that in a book this size, we can't address your every need and concern as a teacher. But we think we give you a good overview, one that we hope will spur you to further study. Gospel Publishing House has many more training resources. They too can help you achieve greater effectiveness in the task God has assigned you.

Last year the Sunday School Field Ministries department introduced a new format in the leader's material that accompanies our staff training books. We have received good responses from those who have seen and used the leader's kit. Once again, we are offering leader's material based on this book in the same format. Each easy-to-store leader's kit contains a student book, a leader guide, and a compact disc. The compact disc contains downloadable versions of the leaders guide in both English and Spanish, as well as a PowerPoint presentation to facilitate teaching the concepts presented in the student book. You can order the leader's kit through your Radiant Life supplier.

As you read, you will be drawing from the strengths of five age-level specialists. We did not homogenize the material. Individual talents, styles, and approaches appear in the various chapters. We hope you enjoy the variety; we know you will benefit from the years of dedicated experience each writer brings to the task.

The contributors to this book are indebted to people in various departments of Gospel Publishing House for the successful completion of this project. We would especially like to thank Natalia Ray for her help in proofreading both the English and Spanish text. We would also like to thank Glen Ellard for his masterful editing which brought a consistency to the work. Special thanks goes to Janet Arancibia for her translation of the text into Spanish. Finally, we would like to thank Donna Swinford for coordinating the technical aspects of this project.

May God use this training tool to multiply the effectiveness of teachers around the world.

Teachers Who Make a Difference

Trust God's Call

By
Wes Bartel

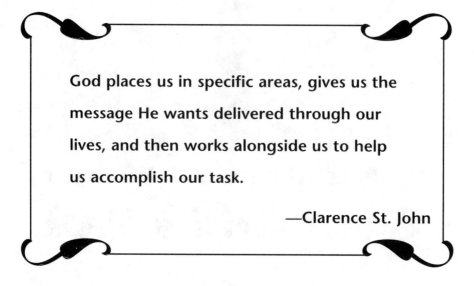

God places us in specific areas, gives us the message He wants delivered through our lives, and then works alongside us to help us accomplish our task.

—Clarence St. John

The scene was strangely reminiscent of race day at Churchill Downs. Fifteen bodies strained forward, intent on the ringing of the bell. When it sounded, they burst from the room, as though released from a lifetime of captivity.

This was the scene each Sunday morning as 15 boys, ages 9 to 11, waited for class to end. The well-deserved reputation of these junior boys sent shivers down the spine of even the most courageous teacher.

The pastor sat quietly in his study and read a letter of resignation from their last casualty. He sighed a prayer for wisdom and asked the Lord of the harvest for a laborer. The class needed someone to feel a burden for these boys and to channel the energy of their young lives. The boys weren't bad. They were just boys! In addition, many of them came from dysfunctional homes where they had learned little about courtesy, obedience, or authority.

But God had brought these young lives into the care of the church, and the pastor felt obligated to them. This obligation was based on a non-negotiable value the church had adopted as part of its spiritual philosophy. Posted in his office and in the foyer of the church, the value read, "Every person has a right to a presentation of the gospel at his or her level of understanding." Now he faced the challenge of finding someone who could make that presentation to the junior boys.

The requirements for the position were relatively simple. The applicant must be faster than a speeding bullet, more powerful than a locomotive, and able to leap tall buildings in a single bound. Unfortunately, the pastor knew of no one like that.

Then, unexpectedly, the pastor heard the Lord speak, laying out His own requirements for the job. They did not include Superman-like qualities. His job description began simply with the word *available*. Whoever fit that description, God would use. Furthermore, the Lord suggested a possible candidate.

Joe was a man in his mid-thirties. He was a relatively quiet and unassuming farmer. He had never taught. The pastor knew that the mere mention of public ministry would create in Joe a reaction that would require a dermatologist. Everyone liked Joe, but no one would have considered him a candidate for a challenge of this kind. However, the pastor decided to act on the recommendation of the quiet voice in his heart.

An appointment was set and Joe appeared in his work clothes with a smile on his face. The pastor prepared himself for the usual response: "You've got to be kidding!" But that response never came. Joe said simply, "You know Pastor, I've never taught a class before and I don't know anything about teaching. But I did decide to volunteer myself to God. Since I told Him I would work wherever He opened the door, I guess I'm your man!"

The pastor prayed with Joe, gave him some training materials to read, and spent the next few weeks working with him in the class. The change was amazing. The boys were enthusiastic, and Joe poured himself into them and their spiritual development. Before long, a class with a history of revolt became a class of budding disciples. Joe became one of the best teachers in the church.

Easter came and Joe could hardly contain his enthusiasm. He invited the boys to his home for a special breakfast. It went well and his excitement was obvious. However, his mood seemed to change in the weeks that followed.

Joe met with the pastor to talk about his concern. With regret he told the pastor that he could not teach the class on Pentecost Sunday; he asked to be excused. "Why?" the pastor wanted to know. It wouldn't be right, Joe thought, since he had never been baptized in the Holy Spirit. He believed the lesson but felt it would be improper to teach something he had never experienced.

The pastor relaxed. Since Joe's problem had nothing to do with belief in the doctrine, the pastor encouraged him to teach the lesson. Reassuring him that "God honors His Word," the pastor told Joe to conclude class with prayer for the students' baptism. Then, he should ask his class to pray that he also would receive this gift.

Sunday came and the pastor quietly breathed a special prayer for the junior boys and their teacher. When class time ended, the pastor noted that Joe's boys were still in their classroom. The worship service began, and the teacher and his students still did not appear. Finally, just before the sermon, the class appeared, and with a smile, Joe nodded to the pastor.

After the service, the pastor learned what had taken place. Joe explained that he had taught the lesson like the pastor had told him. Then he had prayed for those boys who wanted to be baptized in the Holy Spirit, and nine of them were. Then he asked the boys to pray for him. So, gathering around their teacher, these rough-and-tumble boys placed their hands on him. They prayed simply yet profoundly, and God honored His Word. One of them described what happened: "We looked up while we were praying and teacher was swaying back and forth. One of us shouted 'Timberrrrr!' and we all got out of the way as the teacher fell."

Joe celebrated Pentecost Sunday by receiving the baptism in the Holy Spirit. His calling became complete as the volunteer responded to God's special anointing on his life.

Do you want to be a Sunday School teacher who makes a difference? Of course you do! Reading this book testifies to that. However, before we deal with how you can become a teacher with life-changing influence, we must address the unique call and anointing associated with teaching.

Our assignment is non-negotiable and one that must have priority if God's plan for His Church is to be achieved. Jesus said, "Go and make disciples of all nations, baptizing them in the name of the Father and of the Son and of the Holy Spirit, and *teaching them* to obey everything I have commanded you" (Matthew 28:19,20, emphasis mine). The teaching ministry of the church is God's *primary* method of discipleship.

Reasons

What comes to your mind when you hear the terms "teaching" or "teacher" as they relate to the ministry of the church, particularly to that of the Sunday School? In most cases, the picture that forms in our minds relates to a class we have taught or one we have attended. While in most cases there is nothing wrong with that picture, we must probe deeper into its true meaning if we hope to fully understand our task and our challenge.

The Task Defined

Roy Zuck, a noted Christian educator, says, "The gift of teaching is a supernatural, Spirit-endowed ability to expound (explain and apply) the truth of God. Teaching is the gift of systematic instruction and application in the doctrines (or teaching) of God's truth."[1]

C. Peter Wagner, author of *Your Spiritual Gifts Can Help Your Church Grow,* defines teaching as "the special ability that God gives to certain members of the body of Christ to communicate information relevant to the health and ministry of the Body and its members in such a way that others will learn."[2]

The dictionary defines teacher as "one who imparts information or skill so that others may learn." To teach means "to instruct by precept, example, or experience."

Each of these definitions implies the servant nature of the teaching ministry and the role one assumes to carry out that service. As teachers, we have a specific reason for being in the body of Christ.

The Biblical Endorsement of Teachers

Scripture is clear that teachers and the teaching ministry are viewed as one of God's special gifts to the church. The apostle Paul addresses this issue in his letter to the Ephesian church when he says: "It was he who gave some to be apostles, some to be prophets, some to be evangelists, and some to be pastors *and teachers"* (Ephesians 4:11, emphasis mine).

In his letter to the Corinthians, Paul addresses the issue of unity and diversity in the church and closes his instruction by saying:

> Now you are the body of Christ, and members individually. And God has appointed these in the church: first apostles, second prophets, *third teachers,* after that miracles, then gifts of healings, helps, administrations, varieties of tongues. Are all apostles? Are all prophets? Are all *teachers*? Are all workers of miracles? Do all have the gifts of healings? Do all speak with tongues? Do all interpret? But earnestly desire the best gifts. And yet I show you a more excellent way (1 Corinthians 12:27–31, NKJ, emphasis mine).

Notice the lofty status the gift of teaching is given in Paul's list of spiritual gifts.

The Purpose of Teaching

The apostle Paul goes on to articulate the primary purpose of the five-fold ministry gifts listed in Ephesians 4 by telling us that they were given "to prepare God's people for works of service, so that the body of Christ may be built up" (Ephesians 4:12). Just as apostles, prophets, evangelists, and pastors are indispensable to the work of the church, so also are teachers. The role is essential to God's purpose in discipleship.

If the primary focus of the Great Commission is to "make disciples of all nations," then the primary method for accomplishing that task is "teaching them to obey everything" Jesus commanded us. Achieving true discipleship within the church would be very difficult, if not impossible, without the intentional3 development and encouragement of a teaching ministry.

The Perpetuation of Faith

It is frightening to realize that the church is just one generation away from spiritual extinction. On the other hand, this fact provides a stimulus for Christians to do those tasks that carry forward the cause of Christ.

The Bible is very clear about the importance of each generation sharing its faith with the next generation. In the Old Testament, God instructs the people of Israel: "Only be careful, and watch yourselves closely so that you do not forget the things your eyes have seen or let them slip from your heart as long as you live. *Teach them* to your children and to their children after them" (Deuteronomy 4:9, emphasis mine). The principle of perpetuation is a command that God insists be maintained to avoid any generational defection.

The same principle can be seen in the New Testament when Paul instructs Timothy: "You then, my son, be strong in the grace that is in Christ Jesus. And the things you have heard me say in the presence of many witnesses entrust to reliable men who will also be qualified to *teach others*" (2 Timothy 2:1,2, emphasis mine). The need to perpetuate the faith was at the forefront of Paul's thinking, and he understood that teaching was the vehicle to accomplish it.

The Catalyst of Change

A crisis often *initiates* life change, which can result in salvation. However, apart from faith inspired by hearing the Word of God, salvation will not happen.

In the opening lines of the Book of Acts, the writer Luke establishes a two-part plan for moving men and women from natural, human reality into supernatural reality. He writes, "In my former book, Theophilus, I wrote about all that Jesus began to *do* and to *teach* until the day he was taken up to heaven after giving instructions through the Holy Spirit to the apostles he had chosen" (Acts 1:1,2, emphasis mine). The first component of bringing about a life change in people is to live out the faith that you profess. The second component is to transfer that faith to those who need it.

The teaching ministry of the church is, without question, a foundational plan that God himself has put in place. It is His chosen method of accomplishing life change and discipleship.

Responsibilities

We have seen that the teaching ministry and teachers are a high priority with God. He has determined that for His Church to go forward, teachers must be assigned by His Spirit and deployed into action. But to whom has God given this awesome task and responsibility, and by what criteria are they selected?

The Call

Throughout the Word of God, there is record of countless men and women who have been called and gifted by God for distinct purposes. We must affirm that God's plan still involves individuals

15

who respond to a call and become leaders whose life vocation is ministry. I can recall vividly the service where God's particular call on my life was affirmed by the presbytery of my denominational district. I was ordained into lifetime ministry with the challenge, "Preach the Word!"

A misconception of some is that God selects *only* a few individuals for ministry, that the call of God is reserved *only* for someone with unique and special gifts. When people make this assumption, they develop an attitude that suggests only those who have embraced ministry as a "full-time" vocation are qualified to serve God. If this attitude is taken to its extreme, the local church becomes a place for the ministry of specialists. The vast majority of saints are then relegated to the status of spiritual observers. Potentially, this misconception can cripple the body of Christ's attempt to fulfill the Great Commission. If the church is ever to be all God intended it to be, it must return to a more inclusive and biblical philosophy of ministry!

God's mandate for the believer is clear. We are all called to some level of involvement in ministry within the areas of evangelism, service, and discipleship. We each have a call to answer, a task to accept. As a Sunday School teacher, you need to have a sense of calling to your particular task and ministry. You must realize that God authorizes what you are doing and that you remain accountable to Him (1 Corinthians 9:16,17).

The Confirmation

How can you know whether God has called you to the teaching ministry of the church? I believe God will affirm that call in several ways. It may begin with just a growing, unavoidable sense that this is what you should be doing. God may speak to you through others who sense a giftedness in your life and ask for your help. He may also supernaturally reveal His call to you. God usually begins with you where you are. Often, when you are involved voluntarily

16

in an act of service, God will lead you from there to an area of church ministry.

God's army of workers is volunteer in nature. They are people who have been redeemed by the blood of Christ and empowered by His Spirit. They willingly step forward to offer back their unique God-given gifts in the service of the King.

The Equipment

Once you have determined your call to teach, it is the responsibility of leaders in the church to intentionally and prayerfully help equip you to fulfill that role. This responsibility is declared by the apostle Paul in his letter to the Ephesian church. Church leaders are "to prepare God's people for works of service, so that the body of Christ may be built up until we all reach unity in the faith and in the knowledge of the Son of God and become mature, attaining to the whole measure of the fullness of Christ" (Ephesians 4:12,13). Church leaders are not called to exclusively *do* the work of the ministry but to (1) prepare God's people for the work of the ministry and (2) oversee the spiritual growth of the body of Christ.

Preparation

On December 8, 1941, Franklin D. Roosevelt delivered a speech to the Congress of the United States that set into action a war effort unrivaled to this day. Following his "Day of Infamy" speech, thousands of volunteers streamed into military recruitment offices to give themselves in service defending their country.

These young volunteers were not sent immediately into battle. That would have been foolish at best, suicidal at worst! These enthusiastic, zealous young men and women had to submit to preparation and training before they were ready to assume the task of defending their nation.

When we think about preparation to teach, we usually think

about things such as study, plans, creativity, presentation, resources. Such things are very important in successful teaching and many of them will be addressed later in this book. This chapter focuses on topics regarding spiritual preparation.

Spiritual preparation must focus on four areas if the teaching ministry of the church is to result in changed lives.

Embracing God's Purposes

Whenever we respond to ministry needs within the body of Christ, we must begin by honestly assessing our motives. We must ask what drives us. For example, "Am I doing this to meet my own needs, or am I seeking to accomplish God's purposes through my efforts?"

God's purpose for the church's teaching ministry is clearly spelled out by the apostle Paul.

> [The primary purpose of the teacher is] for the equipping of the saints for the work of ministry, for the edifying of the body of Christ, till we all come to the unity of the faith and of the knowledge of the Son of God to a perfect man, to the measure of the stature of the fullness of Christ, that we should no longer be children, tossed to and fro and carried about with every wind of doctrine (Ephesians 4:12–14, NKJ).

The teacher's motive must be to disciple, and his or her focus must be on the spiritual health of the students. Conceit and personal aggrandizement have no place. In Paul's letter to the Galatians he writes: "For if anyone thinks himself to be something, when he is nothing, he deceives himself. But let each one examine his own work, and then he will have rejoicing in himself alone, and not in another" (Galatians 6:3,4, NKJ).

It is imperative as we step through any open door of ministry that we pause for a moment to make sure our purposes are aligned with God's purposes.

18

Appropriating God's Promises

The Promise of His Presence

Just prior to His exit from earth to heaven, Jesus spoke to His disciples and commissioned them. He said, "All authority has been given to Me in heaven and on earth. Go therefore and make disciples of all the nations, baptizing them in the name of the Father and of the Son and of the Holy Spirit, teaching them to observe all things that I have commanded you; and lo, *I am with you always, even to the end of the age*" (Matthew 28:18–20, NKJ, emphasis mine).

What comforting words! The promise of Christ's abiding presence is absolutely essential to the preparation of any teacher. So before beginning preparation, the wise teacher will take time to invite God's abiding presence into the learning process. Why? Because the Holy Spirit is the divine enabler of the teacher!

In the book *The Holy Spirit in Christian Education,* L.R. Bartel states,

"It would seem only reasonable that the same Spirit that prompted men to pen inspired words should be involved in the process of seeking to understand and apply God's Word. The Holy Spirit's presence is not a substitute for diligent study, but an enabler of it."[4]

Paul urged Timothy: "Be diligent to present yourself approved to God, a worker who does not need to be ashamed, rightly dividing the word of truth" (2 Timothy 2:15, NKJ).

The Promise of His Assistance

One Greek word used in the New Testament when referring to the Holy Spirit is *paracletos.* In the King James Version, this word is translated *Comforter.* In other versions, the words most often used are *Counselor* or *Helper.* The Greek word *paracletos* carries the idea of someone coming to the side of a friend to assist or provide aid for them.

19

Whenever the Holy Spirit is involved in the preparation and teaching process, He assists us. He quickens our powers of observation. He helps us interpret the true biblical meaning of the text. He makes the text come alive in ways we have never imagined.

Bartel goes on to say:

> The Holy Spirit is a Helper and Teacher for Christian teachers. The significance of what God has revealed in His Word, insight into its implications and application, and the joy of personal discovery of its truth are all things the Helper does for the teacher. Good teachers, in turn, should pray, plan, and structure opportunities for the Holy Spirit to do this same miraculous work in the minds and hearts of their students.[5]

What a wonderful promise Jesus made to us when He said: "And I will pray the Father, and He will give you another Helper, that He may abide with you forever, the Spirit of truth, whom the world cannot receive, because it neither sees Him nor knows Him; but you know Him for He dwells with you and will be in you. I will not leave you orphans. I will come to you" (John 14:16–18, NKJ).

Being Clothed in God's Power

Salvation

The minimal spiritual requirement for all Sunday School teachers is their individual transformations through the process of salvation (Romans 6:20–23; 1 Corinthians 6:11; Titus 3:5). Those called to teach spiritual truths must themselves know the life-transforming reality of being born again by the Spirit of God!

Roy Zuck writes, "Only teachers who are regenerated by the Spirit of God...begin to qualify to do Christian teaching. To neglect this distinctive is to destroy the lines of demarcation between mere religious education and true Christian education. God's plan is to teach through regenerated personalities whom He indwells."[6]

20

Sanctification

Personal transformation moves from salvation to the process of sanctification, resulting in a more Christlike character, known in Scripture as bearing the "fruit of the Spirit." Christian character is essential to effective teaching. Teachers who really want to make a difference must realize that it takes more than curriculum, methods, and communication skills. It involves a lifestyle marked by Christlike behavior.

Baptism in the Holy Spirit

Before His ascent to heaven, Jesus promised His followers, "You shall receive power when the Holy Spirit has come upon you; and you shall be witnesses to Me..." (Acts 1:8, NKJ).

The baptism in the Holy Spirit is available to all believers and supplies an indispensable power for life-changing ministry (Matthew 3:11; Luke 3:16; Acts 2:1–4). Jesus spoke of being dressed for the occasion of ministry by being "clothed with power from on high" (Luke 24:46–49) —power to present the gospel not only verbally, but also through example. This should not be lost to Sunday School teachers. For them it is both "do as I say" and "do as I do." Christian teachers have an obligation to their students beyond words—to encourage life change by being a role model, someone to observe. As Paul told the Corinthians: "Follow my example, as I follow the example of Christ" (1 Corinthians 11:1).

Being Affected by God's Presence

In the Old Testament, priests and kings were set apart by God and given an anointing for the special task they were chosen to perform (Exodus 29:7; 1 Samuel 9:15,16; 1 Samuel 10:1). Jesus used the term *anointed* when describing what the Father had commissioned Him to do. He quoted from Isaiah and said: "The Spirit of the Lord is upon Me, because He has anointed Me to preach the gospel to the poor, He has sent Me to heal the brokenhearted, to proclaim liberty to the captives, and recovery of sight to the blind, to set at liberty those who are oppressed; to proclaim the acceptable year of the Lord" (Luke 4:18,19, NKJ).

Throughout Scripture the term *anointed* is used to describe the presence of the Spirit of God on the life of individuals who were set apart for service within His Kingdom. Jesus of Nazareth was known as "The Messiah" or "The Christ," which means "God's anointed one."

God still anoints people today and, for a teacher of His Word, it is an essential part of the preparation that goes into one's ministry. If God sets you apart for the ministry of teaching, He will anoint you for that service.

Let me offer a word of caution here. The anointing is not a feeling that comes and goes. It is not something that God gives one Sunday and withholds the next. It is an abiding and lasting reality in the life of the teacher. Perhaps the most accurate way to think of the anointing is in terms of the abiding presence of the Lord. Without question, we sense God's presence working in our lives more powerfully at some times than at others. However, we must reaffirm what the apostle John wrote: "The anointing which ye have received of Him abideth in you..." (1 John 2:27, KJV).

Is the anointing of the Spirit still necessary for the Christian teacher today? It is if the desire is to be a teacher who really makes a difference!

Presentation

Without question, the crowning event for the teacher is the lesson presentation. Effective planning, prayer, and preparation should have placed the teacher in a position where life changes are actually possible for the class members. Now all of the parts come together. The teacher is now dependent on the work of the Holy Spirit to prepare the students' hearts and to empower the words of the presentation.

Lesson presentation is very important. But its effectiveness will be measured in direct relationship to our presentation of ourselves to the Lord. Our effectiveness as teachers is dependent on our moving beyond self-serving attitudes, which often characterize the carnal Christian. Paul sums it up by declaring: "I beseech you therefore, brethren, by the mercies of God that you *present your bodies* a living sacrifice, holy, acceptable to God, which is your reasonable service" (Romans 12:1, NKJ, emphasis mine).

Rely on the Holy Spirit. Then God will take what was once merely human effort and turn it into a divine encounter as His Spirit anoints your teaching.

The teaching task will always be more effective when we present ourselves to the Lord as His servants before, during, and after ministry in the classroom. This act of humility puts us in position to be vessels that can be used by God, who in turn can really make a difference in the lives of our students.

Expectations

For many teachers, the measurement of success is a completed lesson plan. A primary concern heard from teachers concerning their curriculum is that the content is more than they can finish in one lesson. Usually that statement indicates a problem in the area of lesson expectation.

The question regarding expectations that you must answer is related to purpose. What are your goals? What are you trying to accomplish when you teach? Is your goal simply to get through the material, a dissemination of biblical knowledge, or do you have a deeper purpose and expectation for the class or the individual student?

The writer of Proverbs observes: "Many are the plans in a man's heart, but it is the Lord's purpose that prevails" (Proverbs 19:21). Every teacher is driven by something. A driving force or a controlling assumption must be behind what we do. A question that must be uppermost in our minds as we teach is, "What do I want to see accomplished in my class?"

Among other goals you may have, two biblical expectations should be part of every teacher's statement of purpose—evangelism and discipleship.

Evangelism

It is imperative that we intentionally plan our classes so people have the opportunity to enter into a right relationship with God. One of the primary focuses of the church in general and the Sunday School in particular must be evangelism (John 3:16,17; Mark 16:15–18; John 17:18).

From the beginning of the Sunday School movement, the central focus was on the fulfillment of the Great Commission. Its early architects did not believe that Sunday School could function properly without a clear and intentional strategy for evangelism.

Anne M Boylan, in *Sunday School: The Formation of an American Institution* writes:

> The earliest goal of evangelical Sunday School workers was simply to bring religious knowledge, and the behavior associated with it to lower-class youth . . . Although teachers did not expect their instruction to guarantee conversion, they did hope for subsequent conversion among pupils who participated in revivals and believed that Sunday School instruction would at the very least 'rectify and enlighten their consciences,' creating prudent and circumspect individuals.[7]

If we are to be Great Commission churches and Sunday Schools, we must design our classes with evangelism in mind. We should provide an opportunity for people to respond to the gospel of Christ. We should never be satisfied until we can point to individuals who have discovered *in our classes* the reality of a personal relationship with Christ. Our expectation of success should always include conversion.

Discipleship

We build people! Although some will recognize this statement as a ministry philosophy promoted to entire congregations, the phrase represents much more than a promotional campaign. A primary reason for our existence in the kingdom of God is to disciple others, helping to build them up in the faith.

Discipleship can be defined as the process of a person becoming a complete and competent follower of Jesus Christ. It is not a ministry or a program. It is a lifelong commitment to a changed lifestyle. The process involves becoming a committed, knowledgeable, practicing follower of Jesus.

In other words, we should never be satisfied with evangelism only. Certainly a class member confessing sin and receiving Christ as Savior ought to be cause for rejoicing. However, we should always view conversion simply as the beginning of life's journey to spiritual maturity in Christ. Our understanding of evangelism should always include discipleship.

Discipleship cannot occur in a vacuum. It is best accomplished within the care of a church or group of people who are committed to effecting life changes and spiritual growth. Discipleship does not happen simply because we believe in it or because we want it to happen. It happens through effective Bible study, loving care and patience, godly mentoring and modeling, and accountability. These are all components of an effective Sunday School. Furthermore, these components should be non-negotiable for the whole church. By them we become teachers that make a difference.

Evaluation

1. Read David's prayer found in Psalm 139. Then, list your reasons for involvement in the church's teaching ministry.
2. Define in a single paragraph or sentence what you view as your task as a Sunday School teacher.

3. How would you describe the call of God as it pertains to your present ministry?
4. To improve as a teacher or Christian worker, what areas of preparation would you identify?
5. Take time to evaluate your students and their walks with God. Do a spiritual inventory and cite ways you can help them in their growth.

Endnotes

[1]Roy B. Zuck, *Spiritual Power in Your Teaching*, rev. ed. (Chicago, Ill.: Moody Press, 1972), 70.

[2]C. Peter Wagner, *Your Spiritual Gifts Can Help Your Church Grow* (Ventura, Calif.: Regal Books, 1979), 127.

[3]Intentional: "purposely and strategically managing the process that disciples people." This specialized use of the term *intentional* derives from the *We Build People* philosophy, a values-driven intentional discipleship process. *We Build People* resources are available through Gospel Publishing House.

[4]L.R. Bartel, "The Holy Spirit and the Task of Teaching," *The Holy Spirit In Christian Education*, ed. Sylvia Lee (Springfield, Mo.: Gospel Publishing House, 1988), 119.

[5]Ibid., 110.

[6]Zuck, 17–8.

[7]Anne M. Boylan, *Sunday School: The Formation of an American Institution* (New Haven, Conn.: Yale University Press, 1988), 6.

Teachers Who Make a Difference

Model Christlike Character

By
Sharon Ellard

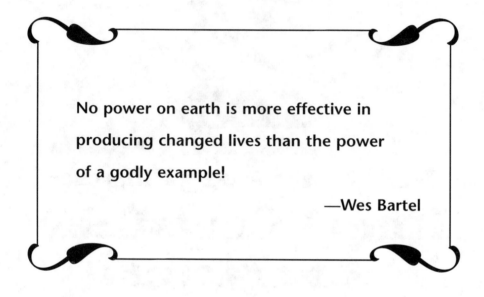

No power on earth is more effective in producing changed lives than the power of a godly example!

—Wes Bartel

Work in an underground coal mine demands people who are almost as hard as the black carbon they extract from the pit. They are individuals who play as hard as they work. And they assume that everyone works and plays exactly the same hard way they do. To many, alcohol and drugs are almost as common as the lunchboxes they carry—a part of being "one of the guys."

Darell Hailey was definitely "one of the guys." To his friends, he looked like any other Joe on the job. He was easy to get along with. He was a good mine mechanic; he did his job well. He had purchased all the "creature comforts" that his paycheck could afford and on the surface everything seemed just about normal. However, underneath was a man who, like a cheap piece of cloth, was quickly coming unraveled. He was spending more than he earned, drinking more than he should, and doing drugs to make it all tolerable.

When news of company reorganization was posted, it fell like a hammer on the mine's employees. Lost jobs and lost hope quickly became part of the everyday cycle of life. It wasn't long before pessimism hung like a cloud over the little mountain town. Darell breathed a big sigh of relief when, instead of termination, he was transferred to the graveyard shift to be retrained as a welder. Life, as miserable as it had become, would go on!

A tall Texan named Billy Joe Watson was the first miner to greet

Darell as he reported for the first night on his new job. Watson seemed just a little out of place with all the others who made their living underground. However, this easy-going, good-natured man had a personality that drew Darell to him almost immediately. What really impressed Darell was Watson's confidence and an air of peace, which was absent from the rest of the miners. Something about him made him very different.

Before long Darell learned that his new friend had two favorite topics of conversation. He loved to talk about the Dallas Cowboys and about Jesus Christ. *Billy Joe Watson was a Christian!* And he really didn't care who knew it! Darell watched and soon learned that Watson's testimony went much deeper than the words he spoke. His life was a model of integrity. His work ethic lifted everyone else to a higher standard. His personal morality contrasted starkly with that of the other miners. To a man whose life was falling apart, Watson's influence was fresh air! Over the next few weeks a very positive relationship developed between the two men. For the first time Darell Hailey was forced to deal with some of the tough questions of life that he had avoided for so long. However, while Darell acknowledged concern for his own spiritual health, Jessica, his 5-year-old daughter, was his main concern. In his own words: "I didn't want Jessica to miss heaven and live in hell!"

Darell's new friend suggested that he allow his daughter to attend Sunday School at First Assembly of God in Grand Junction, Colorado. Darell wasn't sure he wanted to send Jessica somewhere he had never been to learn from people he had never met. Instead, he began to take her himself. Darell would drive to the church and walk Jessica to her class, turn around and leave, and then return for her after services. Even though his contacts were brief, he was impressed by the friendliness and openness of the people.

What was especially powerful was the positive influence the Sunday School teacher had on Jessica's life. Bev Smith had been a teacher at First Assembly for 10 years and took seriously the calling God had placed on her. One night she called the Hailey family and gave Darell a Scripture verse for Jessica to memorize. The verse was John 14:1: "Let not your heart be troubled; you believe in God, believe also in Me" (NKJ). Darell shared the verse with his daughter, but the Holy Spirit shared it with Darell. The impact of that verse on his life was more profound than anything Bev could have imagined. Darell did believe in God; he just had never committed his life to Jesus.

Two weeks later Darell attended a service and responded to a simple invitation by the pastor to ask Christ to take control of his life.

He and his wife, Deon, immediately enrolled in a Sunday School class and began to grow and mature spiritually. Eventually, they assisted in teaching a first grade class and ultimately became teachers themselves. Their growth continued and they were asked to become children's pastors at their church, the same church Darell had entered as a coal miner 10 years before.

Presently, Darell is the Kids Church Pastor of Timberline Church in Fort Collins, Colorado, where he ministers to over 400 children every weekend. His ministry consists of 5 different services on Saturday and Sunday as well as hosting Club 456, a small-group ministry for fourth, fifth, and sixth graders. Today, Darell influences hundreds of children in the same way a man named Billy Joe Watson and a Sunday School teacher named Bev Smith influenced him!

What drew Darell Hailey to Jesus Christ? First, in the coal mine, Billy Joe Watson worked with a confidence and peace that contrasted with the turmoil Darell was experiencing. Second, Bev Smith connected with Darell's daughter. He was impressed when she called with a Bible verse to teach Jessica. The Holy Spirit timed her call so the verse ministered to Darell's troubled heart. God used the Christlike character of ordinary Christians to draw Darell to Jesus.

Once Darell accepted the gift of salvation, he attended Sunday School classes that began to transform his thinking and behavior. Darell learned to use the Bible as a moral compass to guide and protect himself. He discovered and developed ministry gifts of his own. Ultimately, Darell became a teacher himself. Today he influences young students both by the weekly lessons he teaches and by the Christlike character he displays.

Reasons

Anyone who watches TV commercials has seen celebrities endorsing everything from spaghetti sauce to dot-coms. Sponsors pay athletes and actors top dollar to be seen eating their cereal, driving their cars, or wearing their clothes. Top athletes can earn more money posing with products than winning at tournaments. In one year alone, Tiger Woods, who had won $9 million in golf tournaments, earned $53 million making product endorsements[1] —almost six times as much money for his picture as for his skill.

Why are manufacturers and service providers willing to pay so much for endorsements by people who may know (and care) very little about their products? Simply, it is to gain acceptance by association. Sponsors believe that fans who see Tiger Woods eating Wheaties will buy Wheaties in order to feel a little more like champions themselves. In a media-mad culture, paying for celebrity endorsements actually is a good investment. Many people do shop for products at least partially based on who they associate with them.

How do celebrity product endorsements relate to being a Sunday School teacher who makes a difference? First, how well your students will accept the Bible truths you teach depends at least partially on how well you live those truths. Sunday School students expect those who teach God's Word to be living examples of the difference loving, trusting, and obeying God makes.

Second, students learn through imitation as well as information. In this sense, celebrity endorsements fall short. Think about it—are you more likely to become a good golfer by eating the same cereal as Tiger Woods or by being coached by him? Most of us would happily take golfing lessons from Tiger Woods. He's a successful pro, and we would readily place more confidence in his teaching than in his tastes. Do your students see you as a Christian "pro"? Does the way you live give them confidence in what you teach?

Responsibilities

When you agreed to teach a Sunday School class, did you consider putting your life on display part of the ministry description? Perhaps you're wondering if you can ignore this one aspect of teaching. The answer is no. How you respond to the Bible truth will determine what you can expect from your students. Jesus said it this way: "A student is not above his teacher, but everyone who is fully trained *will be like his teacher*" (Luke 6:40, emphasis mine).

Even though you are with your students on a limited basis, never underestimate the ability of your character and your conduct to either confirm or deny what you present in class.

Called to a Lifestyle

Is a lifestyle too much to expect of teachers? Again, the answer is no. It's just the way spiritual mentoring works. Teachers who make a difference understand the truism that who they *are* speaks even more loudly than what they *say*. A big part of making a difference in the lives of those we teach requires living in such a way that they can clearly see Jesus Christ's continuing influence on our lives. One of the reasons Sunday School students should want to be like Jesus is because they can see how following Him is transforming the lives of their Sunday School teachers.

It's a discipleship/teaching pattern set up by God himself. "Be *imitators* of God, therefore, as dearly loved children and live a life of love, *just as* Christ loved us and gave himself up for us as a fragrant offering and sacrifice to God" (Ephesians 5:1,2 emphasis mine). Both God the Father and Christ offer themselves as examples their disciples/students can imitate.

If we want to be teachers who make a difference, we too need to offer our lives as models to imitate. When a teacher can say with the apostle Paul, "Follow my example, as I follow the example of Christ" (1 Corinthians 11:1), that teacher is laying out a pattern for discipleship by imitation. Teaching gains credibility and authenticity when teachers openly practice what they profess.

God Is at Work in Us

Fortunately for us, God is willing to start with us as we are and develop Christlike character in us. Paul describes God's strategy in 1 Corinthians 1:26–29:

> Take a good look, friends, at who you were when you got called into this life. I don't see many of "the brightest and the best" among you, not many influential, not many from high-society families. Isn't it obvious that God *deliberately* chose men and women that the culture overlooks and exploits and abuses, chose these "nobodies" to expose the hollow preten-

34

sions of the "somebodies"? That makes it quite clear that none of you can get by with blowing your own horn before God. *Everything that we have*—right thinking and right living, a clean slate and a fresh start—*comes from God* by way of Jesus Christ. That's why we have the saying, "If you're going to blow a horn, *blow a trumpet for God*" (The Message, emphasis mine).

What a relief—at least for many of us! Even though God does expect teachers to be models of Christlike character, He doesn't expect them to start as superstars with long résumés filled with amazing spiritual feats. God most often recruits leaders (because that's what teachers are) from the ranks of ordinary people.

Why doesn't God go for "the brightest and the best"? He wants His representatives to draw attention to His transforming power rather than to themselves. God chooses tax collectors like the apostle Matthew. He redeems coal miners like Darell Hailey. God wants your students to see His handiwork in your life. God wants your students, based on what they see in your life as well as what they hear in Bible lessons, to leave Sunday School trusting Him to develop Christlike character in them just as He did in you. God should be the featured attraction in Sunday School, not teachers.

Preparation

How does God transform the ordinary "nobodies" He chooses into models of Christlike character? In Ephesians, Paul summarizes the process: "Take on an entirely new way of life—a God-fashioned life, a life renewed from the inside and working itself into your conduct as God accurately reproduces his character in you" (Ephesians 4:24, The Message).

God begins the change on the inside! Through prayer, through Bible study, through the work of the Holy Spirit, He reminds us of Christ and convicts us of sin. These interior changes begin working themselves into our conduct. As we become more like Christ

35

inside, we become more like Christ outside too.

Is There a Resemblance?

Think about the life of Christ. Now think about your life. What similarities do you see? Teachers who make a difference commit themselves to becoming authentic (rather than perfect) models of Christlike character. They represent Jesus by resembling Him. Just by becoming a teacher, you begin to resemble Jesus, the Master Teacher.

Sunday School teachers give up being Sunday School students themselves in order to invest their time and resources in the spiritual development of others.

CEOs recruit one-of-a-kind celebrities like Tiger Woods. Jesus Christ recruits ordinary people; then He transforms them to represent Him so well that people will want to follow Him. This is especially true within Sunday School. Each week thousands of teachers present God's Word to hundreds of thousands of students.

We don't have to be superstars to be authentic Sunday School teachers. Still, how do we prepare ourselves to model Christlike character as we teach Bible lessons that will take our students beyond information to transformation?

Identify Christlike Traits

Back in the Ephesians 5:2 passage, we were told to be imitators of God and Christ. The example of Christ was that He loved "and gave himself up for us as a fragrant offering and sacrifice to God." Romans 12 offers a parallel we can follow as we become like Christ. "I urge you, brothers, in view of God's mercy, to *offer your bodies as living sacrifices,* holy and pleasing to God—this is your spiritual act of worship" (12:1, emphasis mine). Christ died on the Cross as a sacrifice. We are to live our lives as a sacrifice.

But what does that mean? In *The Message,* Eugene Peterson par-

36

aphrases the Romans passage this way: "God helping you: Take your everyday, ordinary life—your sleeping, eating, going-to-work, and walking-around life—and place it before God as an offering" (Romans 12:1, The Message).

Peterson describes this process as a life "changed from the inside out" (v. 2). Sound familiar? The remainder of chapter 12 lists specific ministries and life responses that God considers to be "spiritual act[s] of worship." Teaching is listed in verse 7. God sees your teaching as an act of worship that comes with living sacrificially. Read the following list taken from Romans 12. Place a checkmark by Christlike traits God is developing in your life.

–prophesying (v. 6)	–serving (v. 7)	–teaching (v. 7)
–encouraging others (v. 8)	–giving (v. 8)	–leading (v. 8)
–showing kindness (v. 8)	–holding to good (v. 9)	–showing brotherly love (v. 10)
–being joyful (v. 12)	–being patient (v. 12)	–praying at all times (v. 12)
–sharing with God's people (v. 13)	–practicing hospitality (v. 13)	–being happy with the happy (v. 15)
–being sad with the sad (v. 15)	–living in peace (v. 16)	–being kind to enemies (vv. 17–20)

Today's world needs to see Christlike traits in everyday lives. Your students need to see you imitating Christ with Romans 12 ministries and responses. They are worship, and they are Christlike traits. As you focus on developing these traits in your own life, they will begin to emerge in your conduct where students can see and imitate them.

Presentation

Let's examine more closely how four of the traits from Romans 12 appeared in Jesus' teaching and how you might model them for your students.

Jesus Was Moved by Compassion (Romans 12:15)

When Jesus saw people with needs, He identified with their sadness and responded with compassion.

Have you ever noticed that needs have a way of interrupting our plans—including lesson plans? They did for Jesus. From our human perspective, Jesus was not expecting to perform a miracle at the wedding in Cana (John 2:1–11). He was just "passing through" Jericho when He saw Zaccheus in a tree (Luke 19:1–6). Even when Jesus was tired and planned to rest with His disciples, He was still moved with compassion for the crowds who tracked Him down. He even fed them. From our viewpoint, Jesus had not "planned" to feed 5,000 people, but He saw a need and met it (Mark 6:30–44). Each time a seemingly "unexpected" need emerged, Jesus responded with empathy and compassion.

Some Sunday School teachers struggle when students' needs interrupt lesson plans. I was one of them. I felt frustrated if the needs of my students interrupted the flow of my lesson. After all, I had spent hours reading the lesson and preparing resources. I felt the time constraints of Sunday School—I had basically 50 minutes to get through all the lesson plans I had made.

So if a student arrived in tears (I teach young children and tears happen), I wanted the crying to stop quickly so we could get back to the "real" lesson. I suppose if I had been in an elementary or youth class, students might have wanted to talk about their week at school. Adults might have arrived exuberant or exhausted from events of the week. The life stage of my students was not the problem so much as my misunderstanding of teaching priorities.

My primary focus was on lesson content. Gradually, and graciously, God transformed my understanding to a more balanced view of my role as a Sunday School teacher. God began to help me understand that my students would see my responses as God's responses. If my focus was too much on communicating Bible content, my students might begin to believe that Christianity is more about rules than relationship. When I began to focus on being happy with the happy and sad with the sad, my students began to understand that God's rules emerge from God's love and compassion for His people.

Identifying with students' needs is an important part of teaching Sunday School. Rather than seeing needs as interruptions of the lesson, we need to see them as opportunities to help students begin to see God as a Heavenly Father who always has time for them. When I respond to students with compassionate concern, they see an example of how Jesus wants to respond to their lives. And the truth is, there is always time for the prepared lesson too—even if it sometimes overflows to the next week.

Jesus Was Patient With His Students (Romans 12:12)

We call Jesus the Master Teacher, and He was. Yet sometimes even His best students just didn't get it. They were perplexed by His imagery. Why would it be as hard for a rich man to enter heaven as for a camel to go through the eye of a needle (Matthew 19:23,24)? They were confused by His parables. What did rocky soil and weeds have to do with the Kingdom of God (Matthew 13:1–30)? They misunderstood His goals. When would Jesus throw out the Romans and establish His kingdom on earth (Acts 1:6–8)?

Jesus patiently responded to sincere questions—even when the questions sometimes expressed doubt.

Upon seeing Jesus approach the Jordan River, John the Baptist proclaimed, "Look, the Lamb of God, who takes away the sin of the world!" (John 1:29). Later, though, when John languished in prison, he sent his followers to ask, "Are you the one?" Jesus responded, "Go back and report to John what you hear and see" (Matthew 11:2–6).

How do you respond to students' questions? It's important to respond to them with patience, to create a safe environment where questions can be asked. Why?

First, when students ask questions, their attention is focused on hearing your answer. As questions are answered, not only do students remember more, but they also gain confidence in you as a teacher.

Second, the process of answering questions can promote learning. If you look for answers in the Bible with your students, they will become more skilled and confident in searching for answers themselves. They can also learn how to use a concordance or commentary to find biblical answers.

Third, unasked questions don't go away, they just go underground. Unanswered questions often become the breeding ground of doubt. Teachers who patiently answer questions encourage others to feel confident about expressing their own questions, dealing with their own doubts.

But what if you don't know the answer? It's OK to look for an answer together. It's OK to research an answer for later. It's OK to invite someone to come to your class to deal with the extremely challenging questions. Your patience with questions will help your students deal with personal questions honestly and hopefully. Your patient response to questions displays Christlike character.

Jesus Prayed at All Times (Romans 12:12)

Prayer was a way of life for Jesus. You might even say that prayer was Jesus' spiritual fitness program. He would spend an entire night in prayer (Luke 6:12). He had locations where His followers knew He would go to pray (Matthew 26:36,47; Luke 22:39). His disciples saw Jesus' prayer life and asked Him to teach them to pray (Luke 11:1).

As Sunday School teachers who represent Jesus, we need to pray, just as Christ did. Prayer acknowledges our dependence on God. Prayer opens our spiritual channels and makes us aware of the Holy Spirit's guidance in our teaching ministry. We may not always know our students' needs or how God is working in their lives, but the Holy Spirit does. Through prayer, God makes the connection. Bev Smith did not know what was happening in the life of Darell Hailey, but the Holy Spirit used her faithfulness in teaching Bible verses to draw Darell to the One who could calm his troubled heart with belief in Jesus. Through prayer, the Holy Spirit can connect your teaching routines to the life needs of your students.

So pray. Pray with your class, acknowledging the presence of the Holy Spirit and His role in teaching the students. Pray before class. Arrive early and ask the Holy Spirit, who is always present, to make His presence felt during the lesson. Invite Him to interrupt, if that is His plan, or to redirect the lesson as He sees fit.

Pray during the week. Ask God to shape you to minister to His children. Ask God to shape students' lives to flow with the Bible lessons. Ask God to keep you alert to resources that can tailor the lesson for your church and community. Ask Him to help you find a way into the lives of people when there seems to be no way. Pray that He will raise your expectations of what He can accomplish as you depend on Him.

Tell your students that you pray. They will see you pray in class. Tell them about your prayers during the week too. Sometimes you might send an e-mail to let them know you are praying for them. Sometimes you might make a phone call. Jesus' disciples saw Him pray. Allow your students to see the role that prayer plays in your life.

Jesus Lived in Peace With "Everyone" (Romans 12:17–20)

Jesus lived among His students. They saw His response to all kinds of people. They saw how He talked with social outcasts. (See John 4 when Jesus meets the woman at the well.) The disciples saw Jesus volunteer for tasks they didn't want to do themselves. (See John 13:4,5 when Jesus washes the disciples' feet.) They saw how Jesus responded to skepticism, even when it came from one of His own disciples after His death on the cross. (See John 20:24–28, when Jesus invites Thomas to touch His scars.) They saw Jesus forgive them after they betrayed Him. (See Matthew 28:8–10 when the resurrected Jesus sends word to His disciples to meet Him in Galilee.)

We too live among our students—both inside and outside of our Sunday School rooms. Our lives teach, right along with our words. Our students see how we respond to unappealing tasks, to persistent skeptics, and to friends who "betray" us in some way.

Smile! You're on *Candid Camera!*

No kidding! It's like being on *Candid Camera* 24/7. Someone could be watching at almost any moment. (Am I the only one feeling just a little self-conscious?)

Having our lives on display is one of the top motivators for developing a consistent prayer life. Why? Because consistent prayer keeps us aware of God's Spirit in us, changing us from the inside out. When we are alert to His presence in our everyday lives, the Holy Spirit can push our pause button when some event might otherwise trigger an automatic un-Christlike response. In that momentary pause, we can ask for a response that is better than our norm. Having already committed our day to God in prayer, we can now zip a quick request for a Christlike response for this moment—a response that doesn't come from our nature, but from God in us.

Prayer also helps us avoid paranoia. Rather than being concerned about how others view us, we're focused on how God is changing us. We respond with God's will in mind, and we depend on His Spirit to manage our responses, which takes us right back to our role as teachers in the first place—to draw attention to God's presence in this world.

The next thing we know, we're reporting our spiritual wrestling matches to our Sunday School students—just in case they weren't eyewitnesses. We actually want them to know how God has redirected our daily lives. Knowing how God is helping us gives our students hope that God will help them too. This kind of sharing doesn't glorify us (considering how we would have normally responded), but it does glorify God in us.

Expectations

Jesus was a teacher who made a difference in the lives of His students/disciples. Although He didn't teach Sunday School, He taught something like Sunday School. Jesus preached to large groups, sometimes running into the thousands, but He also gathered around Him a small, diverse group of men and women. He revealed himself more completely to this functional equivalent of a Sunday School class.

The smaller group of men and women was more influenced by Jesus than the large crowds. Jesus revealed more of himself to His "Sunday School class." They saw how Jesus acted when He was sad, angry, and tired as well as when He was preaching, teaching, and healing. As His disciples watched, they sometimes wondered, "Why did He do that?" When they would ask, Jesus usually would explain, because they were His disciples, not the crowds, who came as much to be fed as to be led. The smaller group of disciples would eventually adopt Jesus' new way of thinking and living.

Sunday School should be like the smaller group Jesus taught. The smaller group of disciples could know Jesus better and be influenced by Him more. How about your Sunday School class? Do your students know you better than they know any other church leader? Do you show-and-tell them on a regular basis how Jesus has changed, and is changing, your life? Or do you treat your Sunday School class like a lecture hall, sharing information but not yourself?

Sunday School is the most widespread small group Bible study setting in the United States. According to George Barna,[2] more than 9 out of 10 churches in this country include a Sunday School. In the U.S. Assemblies of God alone, 120,000 members teach biblical principles in groups of 5, 10, or 25, adding up to almost one million students a week in Sunday School.[3] What if every teacher took his or her small group of students to heart as much as Jesus did His small group of disciples? What do you think would happen spiritually?

Evaluation

1. How are the students in your Sunday School class affected by your life? Do they want to be like Jesus because they can look at you and see an example of how following Him changes lives in the world of the twenty-first century? Jesus, who paid His life to save us, has commissioned us to represent Him. Do we live in a way that makes the price He paid a good investment?

2. What Christlike traits is God developing in you that would make a difference in students' lives if they imitated them?

3. What personal traits do you need to ask God to transform in order to become a better role model for your students?

4. Are you authentic with your students? Do you share tales of your spiritual journey? Do you tell them of relationships Jesus is healing, of weaknesses He is strengthening, of prayers He has answered?

5. Do your students find hope for their own lives as they see Christ at work in yours?

Your Christlike character can be just as much a witness for Jesus as the lessons you teach. Take time to evaluate both how well you model Christlike traits and how well they are being transferred to your students.

Romans 12 Trait	Jesus	Me	My Students
serving	YES!	❑ yes ❑ some ❑ not yet	❑ yes ❑ some ❑ not yet
encouraging others	YES!	❑ yes ❑ some ❑ not yet	❑ yes ❑ some ❑ not yet
holding to good	YES!	❑ yes ❑ some ❑ not yet	❑ yes ❑ some ❑ not yet
showing brotherly love	YES!	❑ yes ❑ some ❑ not yet	❑ yes ❑ some ❑ not yet
being joyful	YES!	❑ yes ❑ some ❑ not yet	❑ yes ❑ some ❑ not yet
being patient	YES!	❑ yes ❑ some ❑ not yet	❑ yes ❑ some ❑ not yet
praying at all times	YES!	❑ yes ❑ some ❑ not yet	❑ yes ❑ some ❑ not yet
sharing with God's people	YES!	❑ yes ❑ some ❑ not yet	❑ yes ❑ some ❑ not yet
practicing hospitality	YES!	❑ yes ❑ some ❑ not yet	❑ yes ❑ some ❑ not yet
being happy with the happy	YES!	❑ yes ❑ some ❑ not yet	❑ yes ❑ some ❑ not yet
being sad with the sad	YES!	❑ yes ❑ some ❑ not yet	❑ yes ❑ some ❑ not yet
living in peace	YES!	❑ yes ❑ some ❑ not yet	❑ yes ❑ some ❑ not yet
being kind to enemies	YES!	❑ yes ❑ some ❑ not yet	❑ yes ❑ some ❑ not yet

Endnotes

[1]Robert Sullivan, Venus Eskenazi, Mike Williams "Show Them the Money," *Time,* Vol. 156, Issue 23, (December 4, 2000), 63.

[2]Barna Research Group, Ltd. (1997). *Barna Survey Reveals Current Statistics on Protestant Churches,* [Online]. Available FTP: www.barna.org

[3]ACMR (Annual Church Ministries Report) 1999 Sunday School Statistics. Information available from the Statistician's Office, General Council of the Assemblies of God, Springfield, Missouri.

Teachers Who Make a Difference
Know Their Students

By
Sharon Ellard

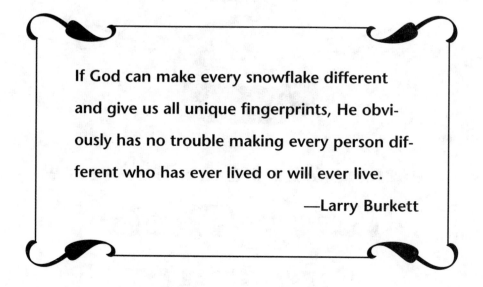

If God can make every snowflake different and give us all unique fingerprints, He obviously has no trouble making every person different who has ever lived or will ever live.

—Larry Burkett

Tonia, Amanda, Bradley, and Sharon—four individuals, four responses, one family.

Tonia came first. She always came, always helped, always learned. A school friend had invited Tonia to Wednesday night girls' club at King's Chapel in Springfield, Missouri. Tonia enjoyed the teacher and new friends. She liked the learning activities and games on Wednesdays, so she began coming to Sunday School too.

Soon her little sister, Amanda, joined her. While Tonia seemed at ease with everyone, Amanda was a little shy. Her eyes might sparkle as she participated in a Bible verse game or action song, but she rarely spoke. While other kindergartners hugged their teacher, Amanda hung back at first. One Sunday School lesson focused on building the tabernacle, a "tent church." Amanda helped to cover a table with a sheet like the tent church. When the class sat together under the table to pray, Amanda prayed that her mother would find a new job. A few weeks later, she came to class talking happily—God had answered her prayer.

Bradley followed. He was the youngest and the only boy in the family. Sometimes he hung near the door as if to say, "They might bring me here, but I don't have to like it." Once, he even hid his head under his coat like a little turtle. Still, it was hard for a 3-year-old to resist gummi worm snacks and colorful stickers. Sometimes his teachers even used balls and sand to teach a Bible lesson. The class included boys the same age as Bradley along with men who joined them in songs, in Bible verse games, and even in crafts. More and more often Bradley walked right in—ready to see what his Sunday School teachers had planned for this lesson.

Sharon came last. She came because her children came. They had grown to love this church and begged to come every week. If Sharon's work schedule caused the kids to miss church, they complained—loudly. As a single mother raising three children, Sharon's life was challenging. She worked hard. She had gone back to school. She wanted to offer her children a better life than she had experienced herself while moving from one foster home to the next. If her children liked this church, maybe there was something here for her as well.

Before long Sharon did find her own place in the church and in Sunday School. Two church friends gave her a surprise birthday dinner to help make up for the ones she'd missed as a child. When her car broke down or one of the kids was sick, Sharon knew that someone would be praying. The people really seemed to care for one another and for her family. They weren't perfect, but they did care.

We all know that even within one family each member is different. Each responds to new experiences in different ways. Each learns in different ways. Each has different abilities and different challenges. Each is at a different stage of life. When people come to Sunday School, they bring their differences with them—hoping to find acceptance, learn truth, and encounter God.

Within His "Sunday School class" of 12 men, Jesus found differences too. He responded to His students as individuals. For Peter, Jesus was ready to repeat himself three times if necessary to be sure Peter heard, understood, and responded. Jesus may have kept a close eye on Matthew the tax collector and Simon the Zealot. One had collected money to support the Roman occupation; the other would have liked nothing better than to throw all Romans out of the country—dead or alive. It wasn't uncommon for Jesus to referee noisy discussions between His disciples—perhaps especially the brothers James and John. Someone nicknamed James and John "Sons of Thunder." Jesus saw the doubts of Thomas, the service of Andrew, the plots of Judas.

Yes, Jesus knew and understood the unique traits of each of His students. In Jesus' mind, knowing His students well was an important factor in being a good teacher.

Reasons

In John 10:1–5, Jesus compares himself to a Good Shepherd. A substitute might be able to tell the rams from the lambs, but for the most part one ewe looks pretty much like the next. Yet in John 10, the Good Shepherd calls each sheep by name and knows if the correct sheep has responded. He cares about all His sheep and doesn't leave even one ewe behind. When all are gathered around

Him, He leads the way from where they are to where they need to be—in green pastures and beside still waters. The sheep follow. They have confidence that the Shepherd (unlike a stranger—from whom they would flee) knows them, is aware of their needs, and will take care of them.

Knowing Our Students
Imitates Jesus' Model of Teaching

Jesus compared himself to a Good Shepherd, but of course He didn't come to die for sheep. He came for people. In His eyes, people wanted to be treated with the kind of individual care that a good shepherd would offer his sheep. When they received that kind of personalized care, they would follow where their teacher led and believe what their teacher taught.

People still respond positively to leaders/teachers who care enough to get to know them. Very early people seem to be able to tell the difference between general greetings ("Good to see you") and personalized interest ("How did the big report go last week?"). Whether they are 1-year-old or 50-years-old, they are longing for people who take time to get on their level, both physically and relationally, and speak with them face to face. They appreciate someone who not only asks for their name but also remembers it the next time they meet. They willingly develop a relationship with the person who recalls their fondness for teddy bears, football, or chocolate chip cookies. The person who naturally works genuine comments about those favorites into conversations (or shares samples) may become a friend for life.

Not only is this kind of individual attention pleasing for the recipient, it's also central to discipleship. In the church of Jesus Christ, every person is of value and is the focus of ministry. When Jesus gave the Great Commission, He was sending His followers to present the good news about Him to every person at his or her level of understanding.

52

Knowing Our Students
Shapes How We Teach

Very often students' responses, behavior, and learning in Sunday School correlate with other aspects of their lives. Knowing our students helps us know how to pray, how to plan, and how to respond. For example, knowing Bradley's birth order and that he was the only male in a busy single-parent home allowed his teacher to offer empathy and time for him to adjust. Knowing that Sharon had grown up in a series of foster homes and still missed the nurture of being with her own family motivated Sunday School classmates to plan the birthday dinner that helped establish affection within a church family.

When we don't know our students well, it's easy, for example, to misinterpret body language as pouting or unfriendliness. Those kinds of miscues sometimes lead us to ignore or give up on students who don't seem to be responding to our teaching.

Responsibilities

Acceptance and Transformation

In his book *Just Like Jesus,* Max Lucado writes, "God loves you just the way you are, but He refuses to leave you that way. He wants you to be just like Jesus."[1] Lucado's thought expresses a basic of discipleship: We begin where the students are and build from there. In John 3:16, Jesus invites "whosoever will" to believe in Him. Jesus accepted Roman soldiers and fishermen, housewives and prostitutes, young and old, rich and poor. Today's Sunday School teachers must do the same if we want to follow Jesus' model for making a difference in students' lives. Jesus loved and accepted people as they were and then began to work gently within them to make them as He is.

Unconditional love and acceptance are strong motivators of

change. Sunday School teachers who know and accept their students just as they are lay a sound foundation. Jesus looked at a big fisherman called Simon, who acknowledged being "a sinful man." Of course Jesus saw Simon as he was. But He also had His eye on what Simon could become. All it would take was being transformed by Jesus' teaching and God's Spirit. So rather than lecture Simon about his shortcomings (and there were several), Jesus recruited him as a disciple and changed his name to Peter, which means "rock." Various Bible scholars have offered explanations of what Jesus meant when He said, apparently talking to Peter, "On this rock I will build my church." Here's one more possibility: Perhaps Jesus meant "I can take ordinary people like this man, fill them with My Spirit, transform them as they follow Me, and build a worldwide church of little rocks like this Peter."

As Sunday School teachers, we continue to empower ordinary people for devoted service to Christ. When we know and accept our students as they are and then project what they can become as followers of Jesus, we encourage them to pursue that goal.

Become Informed

Admittedly, it was easier for Jesus to know His students/disciples thoroughly. Not only did He live with them day in and day out, but He was also the Son of God. For example, Jesus knew Andrew had been sitting under a tree just before Andrew came to Jesus. Jesus knew that Judas would betray Him and Peter would deny Him. His Father God gave Jesus insights beyond human capability.

Still, as Bible teachers we can and should learn about our students if we want to be like the Good Shepherd—if we want to know our students well enough to make a difference in their lives.

In the last few decades much research has produced books that can help us tailor Bible lessons to how various students learn best—whether babies, children, teens, or adults. These books provide insight into God's design of people. Both teachers who have taught for years and those only now entering teaching can become better informed about how people learn.

Why go to the trouble of acquainting ourselves with learning traits? We do it so no student will be left behind when it comes to spiritual development. Based on the Bible, we know that some will be left behind, but it should never be because they were not taught God's Word in a way they could understand.

Preparation

The students we teach in Sunday School come with an amazing combination of traits. Here are a dozen factors that influence the learning process.

Age-level Traits	Temperament	Learning Modes
Life Stages	Life Experiences	Intelligences
Church Experiences	Gender	Generational Traits
Birth Order	Cultural Backgrounds	Learning Styles

Training books, magazine articles, and multimedia resources dealing with learning factors could fill a library. In this section, we'll highlight two and touch on how they should affect our preparation to disciple our students in Sunday School.

Age-level Traits

Without training, we tend to teach the way we were taught. If we primarily remember being taught in elementary grades, we may unconsciously use elementary techniques even when teaching adults or babies. With age-level training, we can modify our teaching preparation to match the age group we are discipling.

Gospel Publishing House has produced a series of colorful training booklets called *StepONE, A Guide for Teachers.* Each 16-page booklet focuses on one age level in order to guide teachers as they prepare Bible lessons for their students. The following are excerpts from the series.

"Adults see themselves as self-directed and expect others to view them that way also. Adults want to decide for themselves what they will learn, when they will learn it, and how they will go about it. The teacher and adult student see each other as equals in a mutually helpful relationship."[2]

"At the heart of youth ministry, relationship must permeate all you do with students if you are to have significant influence on their lives spiritually. Your life may bridge a gap between Christ and students, paving the way to a deeper relationship with Him. Even so, your class' ultimate effect on students will have much to do with their relationship to you."[3]

"Children can be noisy and boisterous. High energy levels are the norm for elementary children. Successful teachers plan ways to channel their students' energy into meaningful activity....Establish effective classroom routines. Children need something to do when they first arrive. Plan an early bird activity."[4]

"Young children learn by doing. The more of their senses they use, the more they will remember. Plan lessons that allow children to touch, taste, and smell, as well as see and hear. During a lesson about Baby Moses, set a tub of water on a bath towel. Let the children float a small doll in a tub. Talk about how God protected Baby Moses."[5]

"Use repetition in your church nursery. Repeat the same lesson for at least a month. As you and others on the ministry team repeat the simple lesson rituals session after session, babies will begin to remember first ideas about God....Celebrate their accomplishment with grins and applause."[6]

Temperament

We are born with a temperament that strongly affects how we respond to experiences, relationships, and information. How others respond to our temperament also affects us, including the extent to which the Holy Spirit can use God's Word to transform our lives.

Some of your students were born with an easy temperament. From the moment they first opened their eyes and gazed on their world, they liked it. When it was dim, they slept. If it was light, they looked around. If people held them, they gazed into their faces and responded to their expressions. If someone laid them down, they nestled in and got comfortable. This easygoing temperament stays with a person throughout life. Most of the time they are equally content in a lecture class or a discussion group. It's okay if their teacher begins with prayer one week and a snack the next. People tend to like them quickly. If they are greeters, people feel at home with them. If they are volunteers for a learning activity, they make it look like fun so others want to try it. Their easygoing temperament is nothing they achieved; they were born with it.

Other students arrive with a slow-to-warm temperament. They don't like transitions—at least they need time to adjust to them. If they are engrossed in building an ark with blocks, they may have a hard time coming to listen to a story. As teens or adults, they may have to sit in the car, convincing themselves to go into the church, then into the class, then into the discussion. They have the potential to either become class outcasts or leaders, depending on how teachers respond to them.

Teachers who don't know about the slow-to-warm temperament may think these students are just being difficult or stubborn. When they're children, teachers may say, "We're waiting for you again. Why do you always have to be the last one?" When they're youth or adults, teachers may give up on them and just ignore them. Classmates notice how teachers treat them and may begin imitating what they see teachers doing. This is how slow-to-warm students can become outcasts.

As teachers, when we recognize that some of our students will be slow-to-warm, we can plan ways to help them feel at home in God's house studying God's Word. If we teach children, we can give them an early alert about when we will change from one activity to the next. We may use a project they're working on as a positive illustration in the next lesson segment. We can establish a schedule to follow every week to make it easier for these children to know what to expect next.

If we are teaching slow-to-warm teens or adults, we can allow them time to feel at ease before involving them in an activity or discussion. Occasionally, we may call them at home and ask them to prepare a report or to appear on a panel. After being given time to think ahead, they may impress us (and classmates) with their contribution.

Slow-to-warm students are less susceptible to peer pressure than their easygoing friends. This trait gives them leadership potential. Since from birth they have taken time to decide their responses (rather than being spontaneous), they may resist a "plot" to disrupt a class, or they may create a better solution than occurs to others for overcoming a challenge. Teachers play a pivotal role in how slow-to-warm students view themselves. We can help them understand how God can use people like them. Sharon's second daughter, Amanda, has a slow-to-warm temperament. Both Sharon and Sunday School teachers accept Amanda as she is, and Amanda has grown into a leader at school.

A third group of students is born with a sensitive temperament. If they're preschoolers, they don't want others to sit too close. If they're children, they may be offended by the way someone looks at them. If they're teens, they may be self-conscious and withdrawn about a slight blemish. Sensitive adults may hold on to a perceived slight for years.

While slow-to-warm students adjust and ultimately become active participants, sensitive students give teachers the ongoing chance to show God's unconditional love, grace, and mercy. As these students feel accepted no matter what, they begin to relax and become more tolerant of others.

According to Matthew 12:20, Jesus "does not crush the weak, or quench the smallest hope" (The Living Bible). Jesus, our teaching model, is compassionate and hopeful about all disciples of all temperaments. When we follow His example, not only do we help students of all temperaments feel at home in God's house, but we also model God's acceptance and love for our students to imitate with one another.

Four Preparation Tips

- Early in the week, between Sunday and Tuesday, scan the lesson for Bible content, lesson goals, suggested methods, and supplies.
- Beside each lesson segment, write the names of students who will be engaged by that part of the Bible study.
- Cross out any segments you plan to replace in tailoring the lesson for your students.
- Pray specifically for your students, asking the Holy Spirit to give you insights into their spiritual needs and interests.

Presentation

Perhaps you're wondering how one teacher can possibly present God's Word for the benefit of diverse students. Variety is the key. A presentation filled with variety will match more of the diverse learning styles represented in every Sunday School class.

Plan efficient ways to include variety in your presentations. Team teaching, curriculum lessons, and the Holy Spirit can help you tailor your presentation of God's Word to the students you teach.

Team Teaching

One of the strengths of twenty-first century Sunday Schools will be the move back to the New Testament model of teaching in teams. When Jesus sent out 72 disciples on a ministry practicum, He sent them out in pairs. When Paul went on his first missionary trip, Barnabas accompanied him. On the second trip, Silas went with Paul and Barnabas took John Mark. In Paul's epistles, he often lists several who are involved in ministry with him.

Teaching teams make it easier to match the learning styles and needs of more students. The exhorting style of Paul was complemented by the encouraging nature of Barnabas.

Teams multiply ministry. Barnabas mentored John Mark. Eventually, John Mark matured into a fine minister whom Paul wanted to join him.

Teams divide responsibilities. According to some researchers, adults in the United States work more hours than the citizens of any other industrialized country in the world. We're busy with work, but we must also continue to be faithful in discipleship and evangelism.

In youth and adult Sunday School classes, teaching teams can divide ministry tasks. One or more teachers can prepare to teach Bible content. One can follow through with pastoral care of class members and plan fellowship events. Another can mobilize the class for ministry both inside and outside of the church.

In nursery, early childhood, and elementary Sunday School, teaching teams can divide up the more intense lesson preparation required to match the age-level need for hands-on learning.

Within any team, some students will be drawn to one teacher while others will be drawn to another. This blending of responsibilities and personalities makes it more likely that all students will connect God's Word with their own lives in meaningful ways.

Your Curriculum Partner

If your class includes a variety of students (and all classes with more than one student do), then published curriculum will help. Age-level curriculum focuses on age-level traits. In addition, most curriculum is also written to connect with different learning styles and modes. Curriculum lessons usually include a variety of content, visuals, and methods to match the needs of different student learning styles, life experiences, and backgrounds. Teachers who choose a mixture of visual, listening, and hands-on methods during lesson preparation will present lessons that match the various learning modes of their students.

Be alert to this tendency: It's easy to fall into the habit of depending on only one or two methods—unconsciously these are most often the ones that fit the teacher's preferred learning style. If you teach with a variety of methods and resources, God's Word will connect with many more of your students.

Often time-constraints won't allow you to use every suggestion in a curriculum lesson. That is perfectly okay. Writers and editors create more than enough ideas so you will be able to pick and choose those suggestions that fit your students, your community, and your resources. As long as you present a variety of visual, auditory, and active/involvement segments, most of your students will benefit most of the time.

Your Spiritual Counselor

The Holy Spirit puts God's Word at work in the lives of your students. "When you received the word of God, which you heard from us, you accepted it not as the word of men, but as it actually is, the word of God, which is at work in you who believe" (1 Thessalonians 2:13). When Jesus promised the Holy Spirit to His followers, He said, "The Counselor, the Holy Spirit, whom the Father will send in my name, will teach you all things and will remind you of everything I said to you" (John 14:26). The Holy Spirit will also encourage your students to tell others about Jesus, so your class will grow. (See Acts 1:8 and 9:31.)

If some of your students are not yet Christians, the Holy Spirit is at work in their lives too. Paul describes this kind of "team teaching" in 1 Thessalonians 1:5: "Our gospel came to you, not simply with words, but also with power, with the Holy Spirit and with deep conviction." As you teach Bible lessons to your students, the Holy Spirit adds power. He also convicts them and draws them to Christ.

You can trust the Holy Spirit to know your students. As you teach, He will apply God's Word to their hearts.

Expectations

The Bible lessons you teach are not to be archived in the minds of your students. They are to transform your students and then to be transferred onto a worldwide web of ministry. All students in your class have potential to say yes or no to becoming devoted followers of Christ. First, they have the potential to say "yes" or "no" to the gift of salvation. If they say "yes," they have the potential to say "yes" or "no" to a life of service. This much may seem obvious, but it's not. According to researcher George Barna:

"Born-again Christians spend seven times as much time on entertainment as they do on spiritual activities."[7]

"Desiring to have a close, personal relationship with God ranks just sixth among the 21 life goals listed, trailing such desires as "living a comfortable lifestyle."[8]

"In a representative nationwide survey among born-again adults, none of the individuals interviewed said that the single, most important goal in their life is to be a committed follower of Jesus Christ."[9]

At the beginning of the twenty-first century, we must raise our expectations of how Bible studies in Sunday School influence our students' everyday commitments and behavior. In order to mobilize students for ministry, we must first know where they are spiritually right now. We must know how to most effectively present God's Word so students understand it, believe it, and live it. We must ask God to raise our expectations of what He can accomplish for His kingdom through Sunday School.

Remember Sharon and her children from the beginning of the chapter? After Sharon became a part of King's Chapel, she began to reach out to families in her neighborhood who needed Jesus. She recruited church members to join her. As a result, vans began picking up children and bringing them to Sunday School and church. Sharon's journey is still in process (just like ours). Sometimes the challenges are big. Sometimes the help seems less than needed. Still, her children have grown spiritually as well as physically, and the family turns to God for His help.

Do you know where your students are in their spiritual journey? Are any of them simply archiving the biblical principles they learn in Sunday School? Have any of them taken God's Word and allowed the Holy Spirit to mobilize them for "works of service" (Ephesians 4:12)?

Evaluation

Paul taught in Ephesus for three years. As he prepared to leave, he gave this exhortation: "Keep watch over yourselves and all the flock of which the Holy Spirit has made you overseers. Be shepherds of the church of God which he bought with his own blood" (Acts 20:28). Jesus is the Good Shepherd. He knows the sheep in His flock. He has called us to be imitators of Him as we oversee His flock. In order to excel as overseers, we must know our students.

(1) How well do you already know your students?

How many students do you teach?

List five names.

When are their birthdays?

What are their interests?

What are their needs?

63

What have you done in the past year to know your students better?

(2) How well do you know their learning styles?

What age level do you teach?

Write three of the dominant learning factors for that age level.
1.
2.
3.

Identify students with the following three temperaments. How are you tailoring lesson presentations for each temperament?

1. Easy

2. Slow-to-warm

3. Sensitive

(3) How well do you know your students spiritually?

How many of your students have confessed their sins and become followers of Jesus?*

How many have been baptized in water?*

How many have been baptized in the Holy Spirit?*

How many students have been mobilized for ministry?*

In the past year, how many ministry projects have your students participated in:

within your church?*

within your community?*

throughout the world?*

*If you teach children, the Holy Spirit will time their commitment to salvation, followed by baptism in water and the Holy Spirit and mobilization for ministry.

Endnotes:

[1]Max Lucado, *Just Like Jesus* (Waco, Tex.: Word Publishing, 1998), 3.

[2]Clancy Hayes, *StepONE, A Guide for Teachers—Adult* (Springfield, Mo.: Gospel Publishing House, 2000), 2.

[3]Carey Huffman, *StepONE, A Guide for Teachers—Youth* (Springfield, Mo.: Gospel Publishing House, 2000), 2.

[4]Verda Rubottom, *StepONE, A Guide for Teachers—Elementary* (Springfield, Mo.: Gospel Publishing House, 2000), 12–3.

[5]Sharon Ellard, *StepONE, A Guide for Teachers—Early Childhood* (Springfield, Mo.: Gospel Publishing House, 2000), 4.

[6]Sharon Ellard, *StepONE, A Guide for Teachers—Nursery* (Springfield, Mo.: Gospel Publishing House, 2000), 8.

[7]Barna Research Group, Ltd. (1997) *The Year's Most Intriguing Findings, From Barna Research Studies,* [Online]. Available FTP: www.barna.org

[8]Ibid.

[9]Ibid.

Teachers Who Make a Difference
Maximize Their Influence

By
Verda Rubottom

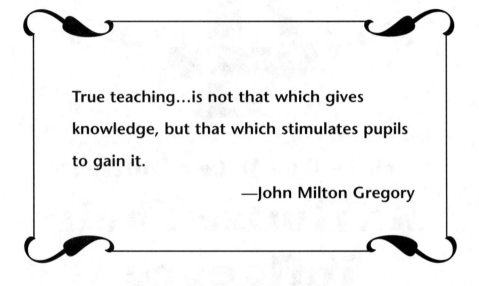

True teaching…is not that which gives knowledge, but that which stimulates pupils to gain it.

—John Milton Gregory

The little town of Staples, Minnesota, is located about 130 miles north of Minneapolis. It has no professional sports team; neither is it the county seat or known as the center of anything. It is just a sleepy, friendly little place whose greatest claim to fame is a boy who became a man.

Guy Rice Doud was born in October of 1953 to Jeanette and Jesse Doud and, by all measurements, seemed destined for failure. Both of his parents were alcoholics and carried with them scars that would undermine not only their relationship with him but his future as well. His mother, Jeanette, gave him all the love and support she could, but she was quietly fighting her own battle of addiction. His father would succumb to dark moods that disrupted and frightened the family. It was a very poor foundation upon which to build a successful life.

In September of 1958, Guy began his formal education at Lincoln Elementary School. It included the usual curriculum of show-and-tell, dress-up days, and learning to read and write. However, the classes proved to be more comprehensive than that. He described them this way: "I was learning a lot more in school than they realized they were teaching me. The most significant lessons had nothing to do with reading or writing or arithmetic, but rather, I was learning about me, about who I was, and whether or not that was good."[1]

It was in those "extracurricular" lessons that he first learned ridicule. Unfortunately it came not only from his peers but also from his teachers, at least some of them. His view of himself grew distorted and ugly. It was as if someone had switched on a flashing message in his brain: "You are not good enough!"

Guy recalls such an incident with a teacher. "I remember getting one of my papers back and on it the teacher had used a can of red paint and underlined my failing grade so many times that I realized not only wasn't I any good at math—I just wasn't any good."[2]

Not everyone treated him this way. Roy Hill and Budd Lindaman, two janitors who worked at Lincoln Elementary School, were kind men who treated the students with respect. Guy learned from their example that you could be happy at your work, and if you were nice to people and treated them well, you could expect a similar response from them.

Then there was Fern Kelsey or "Ferny" as Guy called her. A cook at the school, she also attended the same church that Guy did. Every day he would get a hug and a kiss from her as he went through the lunch line. Her example was a correction for how he customarily viewed himself. After all, if "Ferny" could love him, why couldn't others?

In eighth grade Guy met Mr. Kopka. Despite his thick German accent, Mr. Kopka's genuine interest brought the two of them together as mentor and student. Guy's most enjoyable activity became helping Mr. Kopka after classes. He would often walk by the school at night to see if the light was on in the classroom. If it was, he would knock on the door until one of the janitors answered. He would explain that he had come to help the teacher, and the janitor would let him in. Mr. Kopka would then drive him home when they had finished. Their conversations were open and frank and were guided more by the questions the young man asked than by any agenda of the teacher.

During one such meeting, Mr. Kopka held up a test that he had been correcting. It was a test paper that Guy had completed earlier in the day. "Look who got an A," the teacher said, showing the paper to Guy. "That's a miracle!" he responded. The teacher smiled.[3]

Minutes passed until finally Guy broke the silence with a question that would change his life forever. "Do you believe in miracles?"[4] Mr. Kopka responded affirmatively and then began to speak about the God who works miracles in the lives of people. It was then that he revealed that he had been a missionary in New Guinea. He spoke as though he were a personal friend of Jesus Christ. Guy found himself wanting that kind of relationship also. The teacher never pushed his faith on the boy but allowed his life to become his testimony.

In 1966, the Billy Graham association produced a movie called *The Restless Ones* and Guy attended. There in the theater with his hands full of popcorn, pop, and Milky Way candy bars, he heard the words of the theme song.

There Guy gave his life to Jesus Christ and began a friendship that would become even closer than the friendship he had enjoyed with Mr. Kopka.

Everything in Guy's life did not change immediately. He would deal with the feelings of insecurity and worthlessness that had developed during childhood for a long time. Similarly, the wounds inflicted by people who were poor examples would take time to heal. However, thanks to a teacher who knew the ministry of a good example, Guy's healing had begun.

In 1986 Guy Rice Doud stood in the Oval office of the White House. He had been selected to receive the coveted Crystal Apple award given to the National Teacher of the Year. The President of the United States, Ronald Reagan, extended his hand in congratulations and spoke to him. Guy held in his hand what appeared to be a note card on which he had scrawled the lines to a poem written by Clark Mollenhoff. He read:

You are the molders of their dreams.

*The gods who build or crush their young beliefs of right or
    wrong.*

You are the spark that sets aflame the poet's hand

Or lights the flame in some great singer's song.

You are the gods of young—the very young.

You are the guardian of a million dreams.

Your every smile or frown can heal or pierce a heart.

Yours are one hundred lives—one thousand lives.

Yours is the pride of loving them, the sorrow too.

Your patient work, your touch, make you the god of hope

*That fills their souls with dreams, and make those dreams
    come true."*[5]

The boy had become the teacher...because a teacher had been
his example!

72

In his book *Molder of Dreams,* former Teacher of the Year Guy Doud describes the teachers who influenced him the most during his school years. There were, as he describes them, both the "molders" and the "destroyers" of dreams.[6]

The people who influenced Guy during his school years weren't limited just to the teaching staff; they included the cafeteria cook and the janitors who took time to give Guy the personal attention he desperately needed.

When Guy was growing up, a teacher filled the critical gap left by an alcoholic father. As a teacher, you too have the opportunity to make a difference in the lives of your students.

Reasons

A new generation needs to learn about the God who loves them. But the challenges teachers face today are a legacy of the last half-century in our country: a breakdown in family life and the downward slide of moral values.

Our culture has changed significantly in the last few years, as have the methods available to us for teaching. Yet it is still the caring teacher that will have the greatest effect on young lives. The human need to be valued and loved never changes. This is where we begin when leading people to Christ.

Often, teachers don't see the results of their dedication to teaching young people, but occasionally we hear stories of teachers who meet their former students later in life. Such was the case of Rob Parsons, author of *Almost Everything I Need to Know About God I Learned in Sunday School.*

Rob's parents didn't go to church, but Miss Williams visited their home when he was just four-years-old to ask if she could take Rob to Sunday School. That was the beginning of an exciting journey into the Bible, led by a loving teacher. Miss Williams and other teachers, Parsons reflects, "were not only leading the boy, they were leading the man."[7] Fifty years later, Miss Williams had the joy of seeing him, still walking with the Lord she had introduced him to.

Children, young people, and even adults need someone who will take the time to help mold their lives. Hollywood, Nashville, and Madison Avenue unashamedly compete for a place in shaping the values of people, both inside and outside the church. Don't become discouraged when students don't immediately reflect the Christian belief system that you espouse. Keep taking every opportunity to influence, and continue to pray that God will use your life to help transform the lives of your students.

Responsibilities

Teachers have a wide range of responsibilities concerning the influence they have in the lives of their students. Let's take a look at a few of them.

Responsibility to Families

In the previous example, Rob Parsons' parents may have been apathetic about, or uncertain of, the best way to pursue spiritual training for their preschool son. Unbelieving parents often feel unqualified to talk about spiritual matters with their children, or to choose the right church or Sunday School for them. Whatever the case, it took a woman of faith to bridge the gap between the church and the home in order to lead Rob to a relationship with Jesus.

We too should be alert to opportunities we may have with non-Christian parents who are open to spiritual training for their children. We need to build bridges of communication with the unchurched around us by showing an interest in the welfare of their children. We can be the "salt" and "light" Jesus talked about when we initiate ways to minister to families. To do this may require moving out of our comfort zone and seeking new ways to reach out to lost and lonely people in our neighborhoods.

Responsibility to the Community

Every church should look for ways to evangelize, and to be a dynamic spiritual influence in its community. Jesus gave us the pattern to follow: first Jerusalem, then Judea and Samaria, and then to the ends of the earth (Acts 1:8). It is our privilege—and responsibility—to share Christ first with those in our "Jerusalem." Reaching our neighborhoods with the powerful, life-changing message of the gospel should be a priority of all churches.

One way to pave the way for evangelism is to gain recognition in your community as a family-oriented, or "family friendly" church. This kind of church is known for its hospitality, welcoming people of all ages and backgrounds and serving them in Jesus' name.

When churches and individual believers are involved in outreach ministry and local school and community events, they build bridges of communication with the people in their neighborhoods—many of whom are searching for answers and meaning in their lives.

Our visibility in the community can be a link to the secular world and indicate our sincere desire to share Christ's love with the people in that world. This was the custom of Jesus—to meet people where they were: in the marketplace, in their homes, in the countryside, wherever people gathered. We should do the same, not limiting ourselves to ministry inside the church building.

Responsibility to Encourage Acceptance and Fellowship

People of all ages are looking for fellowship and acceptance. Understanding the unique needs of the people in your class will help you plan ways to meet those needs.

Special events that appeal to children will attract young families. Music and drama will attract teens. Parents and career-minded people want to learn biblical ways of improving relationships and handling real-world challenges in their daily lives. People of retirement age want to feel valued for the contributions they make and for their wisdom and experience.

Finding a place of fellowship and ministry in the church body should not be left to happenstance. Sunday School is one of the best ways to assimilate people into your church. According to Thom Rainer, author of *High Expectations,* Sunday School is the single most effective ministry in closing the back door of the church.[8] This according to a recent study of over 576 Southern Baptist churches and nearly 500 non-Southern Baptist, evangelical churches.

Teachers who are most effective in the process of including people teach their students how to welcome new people into the fellowship. They seek ways to ensure that each person desiring to be a part of Sunday School will have opportunities to enjoy fellowship and spiritual growth with other believers. Evangelizing, instructing, and loving people into the kingdom of God is the heart of the church.

Responsibility to Provide an Example of Christian Living

The effectiveness of our efforts to be a spiritual influence in our community is determined in large part by how we nurture new Christians. If we include them in our fellowship, help them understand what they read in the Bible, and lead them by example, their new faith will take root and grow.

The urgent need in Christian education today is for teachers to be willing to invest in the lives of those they teach and to be living examples of the faith they proclaim. Paul invested in the lives of many and was rewarded with the kind of joy fathers or mothers feel when they see their children grow spiritually as a result of their teaching.

> You yourselves are our letter, written on our hearts, known and read by everybody. You show that you are a letter from Christ, the result of our ministry, written not with ink but with the Spirit of the living God, not on tablets of stone but on tablets of human hearts (2 Corinthians 3:2,3).

Responsibility to Biblical Teaching

Teaching is a high calling and an awesome responsibility. Jesus elevated the teaching ministry by His example as the Master Teacher, and by the standards He set for those who want to teach. "Anyone who breaks one of the least of these commandments and teaches others to do the same will be called least in the kingdom of heaven, but whoever *practices and teaches* these commands will be called great in the kingdom of heaven" (Matthew 5:19, emphasis mine). Jesus reveals to us the importance God places on the teaching of the Word and the honor He bestows on those who practice what they teach.

To teach in a way that will bring growth and change, we need a growing understanding of Scripture that affects and transforms our personal lives. We cannot simply dispense secondhand information and expect to see growth in our students. In order to teach well, we must dig into the Word for ourselves. The Holy Spirit has promised to illuminate our understanding, but we have to do our part by setting aside time for personal Bible study and lesson preparation.

The apostle Paul led by example and went to great lengths to model good conduct for those in ministry. He warned the Christians in Thessalonica about the dangers of idleness, working night and day himself so he wouldn't be a burden to the churches. He set aside his own rights in order to be an example to others. "We did this, not because we do not have the right to such help, but in order to make ourselves a model for you to follow" (2 Thessalonians 3:9).

Paul's goal was to be a model of integrity for those who would follow him in ministry. This can be our goal as well. Though we are imperfect and often need forgiveness, we can be examples as we follow Christ and continue to press forward as Paul did. "Not that I have already obtained all this, or have already been made perfect, but I press on to take hold of that for which Christ Jesus took hold of me" (Philippians 3:12).

Responsibility to Engage in Continuing Training

The need has never been greater for qualified teachers in our churches. We know the influence of a teacher can be far reaching, for good or for bad, in the life of a child. To follow the biblical pattern we must teach by our example, both inside and outside the classroom. To ensure that those who teach our most vulnerable members are living a consistent Christian life, a growing number of churches have adopted a "six-month rule" in recent years. Though we should not expect perfection, the six-month observation period gives leadership time to see whether there is a consistent pattern of Christian living in a prospective teacher.

Teaching positions in the public arena require many years of specialized study and generally include a full year of student teaching under the guidance of a successful mentor-teacher. It seems reasonable to expect those who teach the Word of God to our young people, and thus assume a position of influence over them, to be willing to engage in ongoing training.

Teachers can continue to develop their teaching skills by attending training meetings and workshops provided by the church and denominational bodies. Books and Christian education magazines are also good investments for anyone seriously interested in developing his or her teaching skill. Many excellent web sites are available as well.

Preparation

Like anything worthwhile in life, teaching requires an investment of time. But even more important than this is having a motivation that comes from within. No amount of planning and study will be effective if your assignment is done solely out of duty and responsibility. Enthusiasm—the kind that overflows from your heart as you teach—is the ingredient that will make your students love to come and learn each week. The memory of this kind of relational and inspirational teaching will remain with your students long after the details of your lesson fade.

If you've lost your love for teaching, follow Paul's advice to Timothy to "stir up" (KJV) or "fan into flame" (NIV) that gift of God (2 Timothy 1:6). You may ask, "Just how does one stir up the gift and come into the classroom excited about teaching week after week?"

The key here is to seek God for a vision of what He can do in your Sunday School, a vision of how God can use you to shape lives. This kind of vision comes from seeing people as Jesus sees them, understanding their needs, and believing in God's power to change them. Without such a vision, teaching can become dull and routine. Neither children or adults learn well in this kind of atmosphere, but they will respond to an enthusiastic teacher who shows interest in them.

Next, we can make the most of our influence in the classroom by preparing ourselves spiritually for the task. Christian educator Dr. Howard Hendricks reminds us that we are most effective as teachers when we teach "not just head to head, but heart to heart."[9] Setting aside time for study during the week opens the way for the Holy Spirit to speak to us and illuminate our understanding.

There is no substitute or shortcut for this essential part of preparation. Often it is during these times of prayer and meditation that the Lord gives ideas and answers to perplexing situations in the classroom. God guides teachers today just as He did in the early days of the Church. We can be confident of His guidance as we make our plans to teach each week.

Lesson Planning

Lesson planning is similar to meal preparation. After the menu has been decided, the ingredients need to be gathered, combined, and served in an appealing manner. Reading a lesson to your students from a teaching manual is like reading a recipe from a cookbook instead of serving the prepared food. The teacher's guide provides a list of the essential ingredients—the resources you'll need for a well-balanced lesson. Your part is to pull it all together in a way that will interest and challenge your students.

Planning will be easier if you rehearse the theme and look ahead to see the topics of coming weeks. Write down the topic and theme of each lesson in the coming quarter. Add to your list the memory verses and materials list. As you plan, be alert for newspaper or Internet articles that relate to the lesson. Teachers of children can begin a topical file of lesson review game ideas, object lessons, and puppet and drama skits.

Your Learning Objective

The objective of your lesson is the central truth, or main concept, you want the students to learn that day. For example, if the class is studying the life of Paul and you want the students to learn how he successfully finished his life, your objective could be "How to Keep Your Eyes on the Goal." Keep in mind that your students need to learn the concept and understand how to apply it to their lives. This means you choose relevant life applications for different age groups.

For children, you could illustrate by using a familiar sports theme. Discuss the importance of goals in our lives. Ask the children if they have goals they want to reach. Have them illustrate or write about their goals and, if they would like, share with the rest of the class. Discuss how distractions and temptations can keep us from our goals.

Use objects or pictures to illustrate distractions, and choose games that will demonstrate pressing toward a goal. Select illustrations from the lives of Christian athletes and the training they go through to be successful. Finally, guide children in setting goals in their lives that will bring honor to God. This would be a good time to share some of your experiences with goal setting.

Choosing Teaching Methods

Whatever age group you teach, you will need to decide which teaching methods to use, how to set up your classroom, and the best way to accomplish your overall objective. When I began teaching adults how to teach children, I noticed a distinct contrast between my adult audiences and the children I was used to teaching. I had to adapt my methodology and general approach to suit a different age group. For example, the life experience of adults eliminated much of the need for the explanations I was used to giving to children, and the adults didn't need as many visual illustrations. The energy level in a room full of adults was considerably lower than in a room full of children...and there was no need to go over the class rules to keep order.

The age group you teach will determine the kinds of methods you use, the arrangement of the classroom, and the goals you work toward. Thought should be given to how much interaction you want in the class. It's good to keep in mind the various teaching strategies available and not overuse any one method.

To maximize your teaching influence, use methods that allow for some feedback and discussion of the issues. Greater participation in class will increase interaction between the students and create a more open atmosphere, where people will be able to learn from each other as well as from the instructor.

Studies show that people remember far more when they participate than when they only sit and listen. Furthermore, when people ask questions and discuss issues, they reveal much about their understanding of the subject, or lack of comprehension. This alerts a teacher to offer fuller explanations and insight to the class. It also opens up the opportunity for the teacher to challenge students to search the Scriptures for themselves.

One role of the teacher is that of guide, pointing students to a clearer understanding of a given topic based on the authority of the Bible. However, the teacher should not be expected to do all the thinking. Rather, engage the minds of the students with thought-provoking questions and challenges to do their own searches for scriptural meaning and life application.

Other teaching methods that are effective with junior-age through adult-age groups include panel discussions, small group discussions, dramas and skits, as well as media presentations that are followed by analysis and discussion.

Classroom Arrangement

Your classroom arrangement can enhance your teaching or detract from it. For adults, round tables or chairs placed in semi-circles facing the instructor will encourage interaction and discussion. If you use the lecture method, be sure to have an area somewhere in the room that invites conversation. This could be a refreshment table with nearby chairs or a welcome table where people sign a roll sheet and get their name tags. A small table with books and other materials that relate to the Sunday topic can be a catalyst for conversation and fellowship. Class missions and community service projects also serve to draw people together as they work and plan in small groups.

Children's classes require more planning for room organization and lesson preparations. You can arrange your classroom in a way that will encourage order without sacrificing space while still allowing some creativity and physical movement. A large room can be divided into an area for worship music, Bible story time, and puppet plays, with other areas furnished with tables for pre-session and review games, crafts, and snack time.

Children will adapt to areas that are clearly defined for a specific activity. For instance, young children will enjoy sitting on carpet squares or in child-size chairs (which can be easily moved out of the way for other activities) arranged in a semi-circle for story time. Having ample personal space clearly defined for specific activities will lessen distractions and make it easier for the children to listen. Older children enjoy having interest areas, where they can choose from a variety of activities. Self-guided Bible review games and creative projects students work on together will increase their interest and desire to be involved in learning.

Presentation

When planning your presentation, remember that your presentation methods should flow out of your lesson plans. For example, you may be a skilled puppeteer, but another teaching method may be more effective for the topic you're teaching. One of the benefits of team teaching is having other teachers who can, on occasion, present the lesson using a different method or teaching style. Presentations can also include guest speakers who are gifted in ways that will benefit your class. This will strengthen the teaching ministry in your class, and your students will appreciate the variety.

Keep in mind that presentation includes more than just a teacher-led lecture format. For children, it can involve a pre-session that will require their "hands-on" involvement. For adults, it can take the form of a topic-related time of sharing by various class members that will lead into the lesson. Youth especially enjoy human video and media presentations.

Your presentations can involve a variety of methods, but whatever the age group you're teaching, presentations should include certain key elements. Your presentation should appeal to the age group you're teaching and should be communicated in a format they can clearly understand and relate to. Using visuals almost always increases your effectiveness. Choose your illustrations carefully to support your message and not just because they will grab the attention of the audience. Otherwise, an illustration may distract your students from your objective and they could miss the whole point of the lesson.

Expectations

When teachers ask God to use their efforts, gifts, and talents, they can rest assured that God will be there to help them. Remember the story of Moses. Though well educated in the house of Pharaoh, Moses felt inadequate for the job God had called him to do. God used Moses' rod, previously used to guide sheep in the desert, to lead a great people to the Promised Land. We should be encouraged by this remarkable story, not by comparing ourselves to Moses but because God can use any man, woman, boy, or girl who is willing to be used.

We can be an influence for good in the lives of others if we allow the Holy Spirit to work through us as we teach. Ask yourself the following questions each time you teach. Then ask the Lord to enable and anoint you as you minister in Jesus' name.

Evaluation

1. Do I look for ways to encourage individual students in my class?
2. In what ways do the members of my class extend themselves to include new people in activities both inside and outside of class?
3. How does our class reach beyond the church building to influence those in our community?

4. How am I developing the teaching gifts God has given me?

5. Do I evaluate my effectiveness as a teacher on a regular basis?

6. Do I seek new ways to minister more effectively?

Endnotes

[1]Guy Rice Doud, *Molder of Dreams* (Pomona, Calif.: Focus on the Family, 1990), 52.

[2]Ibid., 56.

[3]Ibid., 83.

[4]Ibid., 83.

[5]Ibid., 84.

[6]Ibid., 7.

[7]Rob Parsons, *Almost Everything I Need to Know About God I Learned in Sunday School* (Nashville, Tenn.: Thomas Nelson, 1999), xi.

[8]Thom S. Rainer, *High Expectations* (Nashville, Tenn.: Broadman and Holman Publishers, 1999), 29–47.

[9]Howard Hendricks, *Teaching to Change Lives* (Sister, Ore.: Multnomah, 1987), 81.

Teaching That Makes a Difference

Sets a Measure for Maturity

By
Clancy P. Hayes

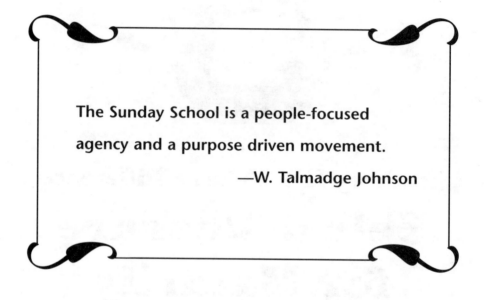

The Sunday School is a people-focused
agency and a purpose driven movement.

—W. Talmadge Johnson

The scene appeared almost dreamlike to the pastor as the Sunday morning unfolded. The church was packed and ushers were scurrying about setting up folding chairs and finding places for visitors to sit. The worship team seemed especially anointed and the entire congregation was deeply involved in adoration and praise to the Lord. Even the special music was without the glitches and sour notes characteristic of past presentations. The pastor was extremely gratified as he watched the lay leaders and deacons of the church glance around and then, with an enthusiastic smile, immerse themselves in this newfound excitement.

It hadn't always been this way. The church had suffered enough splits, discontent, and financial reverses in past years to destroy most congregations. At the same time, it had developed a reputation in the community that was anything but positive, and the remaining members had almost given up hope that the church could ever recover. The dreams and vision they had when the church first began faded to a wistful hope for survival.

Now the dreams were returning. And the pastor leaned back with a smile of his own and wondered what the future held for this congregation. The big question echoing in his mind was no longer about survival but "Just how big can this church become?" He knew from experience that an indispensable ingredient of church growth is momentum, and now that the church had that ingredient, he intended to stir the pot with all his might!

Everything had come together at just the right time. They had retired the church mortgage just two years before and were now debt free. Their building was large and they still had more than enough room for expansion. Even the people most bitter about the past had finally buried the hatchet and were in unity with the rest of the congregation. They had expressed their love for the pastor and his family and had begun to show a willingness to follow his leadership. In the pastor's opinion, the only limiting factor in continued growth was the size of their vision.

Then God appeared! His presence was not visible nor was His voice audible, yet He was there, and the pastor could sense it. A whispered conversation ensued in his heart that would change his life and his ministry forever.

"Son," God spoke. "You've asked the wrong question. Thus, you arrive at the wrong conclusion."

The pastor responded, "Then what is the right question?"

The response from God was one of priority and purpose. "Your question should be, 'What kind of product is the church producing?'"

As the pastor's eyes scanned the congregation, he began to understand. He saw couples still struggling with relationship issues that should have been resolved long ago. He saw continued immaturity in many members who had been a part of the church for years, yet remained unaffected by its message. He also knew of many (some were even church leaders) whose honesty and financial dealings in the community were questionable.

It dawned on the pastor that if the true success of the church is to be judged, as God had said, by the product it produces then perhaps his priority for the future should be the development of his people into mature Christians. For him, the issue suddenly became clear. *Ministry that really makes a difference must have as its priority life transformation and spiritual maturity.* His biblical responsibility and the responsibility of the church was to create an environment that encouraged spiritual growth, confronted spiritual decline, and fostered spiritual maturity (Christlike behavior and attitude).

The true success of this pastor's work would no longer be measured by the traditional criteria of bodies, bucks, and buildings. It would have to be measured by helping individuals mature into disciples of Jesus who experience the joy and fulfillment of making a difference in the lives of others.

The time and energy teachers invest in their ministries should result in transforming their students. But what should that transformation look like and how can you measure it to determine if it corresponds with what God wants?

It is important to determine the reasons for what you're wanting in your students, to discover your responsibility in bringing about these desires, and to find ways to help these things happen in their lives. In this chapter, you will find practical suggestions that will help you achieve those goals.

Reasons

The reasons for setting measurable goals for the transformation process are multifaceted. Space does not permit the presentation of an exhaustive list of reasons for measurable goals, but the rationale given here will provide an overarching representation of reasons for this vital aspect of your ministry to students of all ages.

The Biblical Mandate

The primary reason for monitoring your students' growth as disciples is because the Bible says to. The work of teachers, along with other leaders in the church, will be judged according to the standard outlined in Paul's letter to the Ephesians.

> It was he who gave some to be apostles, some to be prophets, some to be evangelists, and some to be pastors and teachers, to prepare God's people for works of service, so that the body of Christ may be built up until we all reach unity in the faith and in the knowledge of the Son of God and become mature, attaining to the whole measure of the fullness of Christ (Ephesians 4:11–13).

You can do many important things as a teacher. But in the end your work must transform your students spiritually; otherwise, you have touched only the natural part of them. Without question information is important (Romans 10:14). However, the accumulation of knowledge alone is a futile goal for one who teaches the Word of God (Romans 2:13).

What separates you as a teacher in the church from the teacher in the public school is your responsibility to help your students apply the material you are teaching them. It is not enough to present cognitive information that they will be able to repeat on some sort of examination. Although biblical literacy is important, it is not enough. Thousands of agnostics in our world today have more knowledge of the Bible than many mature Christians. When God does our final job evaluation, His highest marks will be for those who tried to help their students grow in all aspects of their spiritual lives.

The Importance of an Intentional Approach

An old proverb says, "If you don't aim at anything, you will hit it every time." Many Sunday School teachers have unintentionally adopted this motto for conducting their classes. They often walk away from class really unsure of why they were there. Sometimes these aimless teachers feel they have been successful if they are simply able to walk away at the end of class unharmed.

If you have found yourself wondering why you teach each week, it is probably time for you to develop an intentional approach to your teaching task. The first step is to recognize the need for having an end view of the maturation process. This must be in place for planning the discipleship steps to be taken in the classroom from week to week. If this is not done, each class session will only randomly contribute to your students' maturation.

Teachers from the nursery to the senior adult class must design each session to reinforce an overall plan that leads students from one level of maturity to the next. Determine what you (and God)

93

want your students to become in Christ. Then develop the components of each class session to lead to that result.

There is more than one advantage to having a long-term view of the discipleship process. For example, it will help you realize that you don't have to fit everything into the lesson every week. One week may be heavily weighted toward exposition of a passage of Scripture. Another week you might spend a great deal of time praying for one another. You may wish to spend a series of weeks on the relationship-building aspect of your lessons. Being aware of the long-term spiritual outcome you're looking for allows you to think in blocks of lessons rather than individual, isolated lessons.

People Respond to Expectations

Were you ever in a pass/fail class in school for which the teacher had no tests or quizzes to hold you accountable for class work? If you had a class like that and were like most students, you didn't put as much effort into it as you did other classes, when you knew your G.P.A. depended on completing the assignments.

People naturally work hardest when they feel that what they are doing is going to be measured. This principle tends to be true in all areas of life, including that of Christian growth. People who have a clear spiritual goal will generally expend more effort than if they have nothing to aim at. If you don't explain your spiritual expectations for your students, you can't really expect much of a return for your time and energy as a teacher.

Clearly describing a path to spiritual maturity will challenge each student to move along in obedience to the commands of Jesus. Students will see that attending Sunday School is more than a social occasion or a religious obligation. They will understand that Sunday school supplies spiritual ingredients which, when combined with other discipleship opportunities in the church, will result in them becoming more like Jesus.

Responsibilities

Setting forth a spiritual growth plan that has measurable outcomes, in effect developing a discipleship strategy, is the responsibility of church leadership. The teaching staff of the church should participate in this. Once the strategy has been articulated, teachers as well as other discipleship leaders should devise ways to make it happen in the lives of their students. Implementing the strategy on behalf of students means teachers must embrace transformational principles.

Teachers and Leaders Must See the Need

Some Sunday School teachers do not see their role in the disciple-making process. If students show up each week and the class gets through the curriculum, teachers feel they have accomplished their assigned task. But teachers must also see their task of having the larger disciple-making goal in mind. Otherwise they will do little to evaluate the spiritual progress of their students outside the classroom, when they are at home, at work, and at play.

As long as teachers and church leaders fail to look beyond the week-to-week attendance figures, spiritual growth will happen only by accident. From time to time, a person will excel in his or her spiritual growth and will stand out in the class. This is the opposite of what should be happening. Spiritual growth and maturity should be the norm rather than the exception.

A teacher can transition from aimless teaching to goal-oriented teaching that produces spiritual maturity any time. But it often occurs when a teacher begins to feel a sense of dissatisfaction with the status quo among the students. Through prayer and introspection, the teacher begins to sense that more should be happening in the students' spiritual development. The teacher then begins to envision every child learning to love more fully or every teen developing a heart of service or every adult fully embracing what it means to be a citizen in the kingdom of God. Once the teacher embraces this vision, he or she is compelled to find a way to make this growth a reality.

Teachers Must Promote the Vision

Teachers must help their students see their potential in Christ. Teachers cannot assume that their students understand the principles of spiritual growth or that they fully understand their responsibility within the body of Christ. Many students assume that sitting in Sunday School and church each week fulfills their spiritual obligations. Those who teach God's Word must not reinforce this mentality.

Promote the vision of spiritual development in each of your students by challenging them to take the next step in the maturation process. For example, posters emphasizing the importance of sharing can be placed in the nursery and early childhood areas of the church. Verbal praise can be offered to elementary children who play together in a healthy manner. Teens can be challenged to make a difference in their schools and communities by expressing their faith in practical ways. Adults can be motivated to discover their spiritual gifts and then encouraged to use them. It is your responsibility as a teacher to continually direct your students to look beyond their own needs; through the spiritual equipment God has given them, they should be meeting the needs of others.

Teachers Must Train Their Students

Training moves a person from knowledge to practice. In many cases, the teacher-trainer will need to walk beside the disciple-trainee, showing just how that knowledge is put into practice. At other times, the trainer must provide opportunities in a safe environment for the trainee's practice of the task. In both cases, it is the responsibility of the teacher to move the student from dependency to competence.

96

Training students takes time and requires a different skill set than possessed by the typical Sunday school teacher. Training is a long-term process that requires a desire to change on the part of the student and patience on the part of the teacher. Jesus himself was willing to invest in this laborious discipleship process, being with His disciples over a three-year period. This itself attests the importance of hands-on training.

Preparation

You have recognized the importance of having goals of maturity that are measurable. You have determined your basic responsibilities for fulfilling those goals. Now you must learn exactly what goals will lead your students to their next stage of spiritual maturity. Preparation to do this requires the following components.

Determine a Biblical Model of Maturity

A variety of models can be used in the disciple-making process. A model that Jesus used can be summarized with four statements from the *We Build People* philosophy of discipleship (promoted in other materials produced by Gospel Publishing House): "Come & See" (John 1:39), "Come & Follow" (Mark 1:17), "Come & Be" (Mark 3:13), and "Remain & Go" (John 15:5, Matthew 28:19).

These four statements have been translated into the following measurable discipleship goals: (1) to help students make a commitment to being involved in a local church, (2) to help students make a commitment to develop an intimate relationship with God, (3) to help students make a commitment to become involved in ministry to others, and (4) to help students make a commitment to become involved in the discipleship of others. Throughout the remainder of this chapter, the *We Build People* process will be used as the primary example of discipleship.

Survey the Available Resources

Once you have settled on a discipleship model, begin looking for resources that will help your students accomplish the spiritual goals associated with that model. Don't tell students what their lives could be unless you are ready to give them a way to arrive there. Doing so will only frustrate students.

Some discipleship models, including *We Build People,* have ready-to-use materials for leading people through the discipleship process. If after studying Scripture you discover a discipleship process that you like better than the *We Build People* process, you must be willing to find resource material that supports it. If you can't, you will have to develop your own. The point is that you must have materials to accomplish the goals that you have determined are important. In other words, you need a deliberate approach to discipleship, and you need to make your students aware of the resources that will help them grow strong in Christ.

Embrace the Role of Facilitator

Teachers who make a difference accept the role of coach in their students' lives. They are not simply dispensers of information. They are facilitators of skills that will mature students in their faith. For many teachers, this shift is difficult; it means they have to refocus from the Bible lesson to students' needs. Although this shift is essential in the disciple-making process, many teachers feel they are being unfaithful to God's Word when they do so.

You are not slighting the Bible by shifting your focus from the presentation of the lesson to its effect on the student. The Bible was never intended to be simply a book of information, irrelevant to the reader's life. The purpose of Scripture is to reveal God's plan of salvation and to transform lives.

As you prepare to help your students mature, include practical examples of how the Bible's information can be applied to life.

Encourage students to provide examples of their own. Be brave enough to share failures, as well as successes, from your own spiritual journey. Doing so will help students stay on the path to spiritual maturity once they leave the classroom.

No, teachers who facilitate spiritual growth do not have to hold the hands of their students. But they must help students set their own goals, encourage their spiritual progress, assess their strengths and weaknesses, help them determine their gifting, confront any errors in doctrine and behavior, and provide opportunities for ministry. Yes, this involves a greater personal investment than what teachers typically expend. But the investment will ultimately yield spiritual maturity.

Cultivate Spiritual Gifts

Teachers who focus on the spiritual transformation of their students understand that they represent a variety of spiritual gifts. Furthermore, such teachers realize that their students must discover their spiritual gifts and be willing to develop and use them in God's service. Doing so is a key component in the spiritual maturation process.

Some teachers concentrate on developing the gifts that are listed in Ephesians 4 or 1 Corinthians 12 because of their "spiritual" nature. But there are many more gifts that Christ has given to His Church. For example, the list in Romans 12 includes some of the more "earthly" gifts, such as hospitality. Teachers should recognize that all the gifts of the Spirit are important and encourage students to develop their gifts—without categorizing them. Many books and gift assessment tests are available to inform you about this valuable aspect of discipleship training.

Presentation

Proper preparation will lead to effective presentation of discipleship goals to your students. Your preparation must reflect the basic values of the discipleship process you are promoting. Here is an example of value statements from the *We Build People* discipleship process. If you choose a different discipleship process, be sure to embrace the values espoused by those who promote it, or develop value statements that are consistent with it.

Overarching *We Build People* Value Statement

"Every person is valued and the focus of our ministry."[1]

"While there are many models and potential structures for ministry, the principle of the individual must become non-negotiable. Church history has proven that culture and sociological trends may impact the program or style of the church, but the requirement that individual life-change be central is a timeless absolute.

Nowhere is the priority of the individual more vivid than in the life and teaching of Christ. He established a pattern both for His disciples and for His church today. That pattern focuses clearly on the needs of and ministry to the individual."[2]

We Build People Value Statement # 1

"Every person has the right to a presentation of the gospel at his or her level of understanding."[3]

According to the architects of the *We Build People* philosophy, "The emphasis is on the individual's level of understanding. The statement does not accept a blanket presentation of the gospel. Only a tailor-made effort is acceptable."[4]

This commitment to tailoring the lesson to the needs of the individual students in your class is enormous. It demands that you know each of your students and that you care enough about them as individuals to include a variety of methodologies to meet their needs. It also demands that you become aware of the developmental needs of your students. Fortunately, this latter information can be gleaned from a number of resources, including the *Here's How* videos available through Gospel Publishing House.

We Build People Value Statement # 2

"Every person needs a biblical, moral compass to guide and protect him or her throughout life."[5]

A basic presupposition of any teacher in the church is that the Bible is life's central authority. In addition, teachers must also believe that the Bible offers clear direction for the Christian's day-to-day life. When teachers make this a key part of their personal philosophies they are more apt to see the need to communicate and demonstrate this truth for their students.

Another important part of this value statement is the recognition that learning is a process. The school of the Bible is not over after a set number of courses have been completed. In essence, we never graduate until the Master calls us to the eternal "commencement ceremony," when our efforts will be rewarded. As teachers, our job is never finished. And we will never run out of material to teach as long as there are ever-changing students in our classrooms.

We Build People Value Statement # 3

"Every believer has unique gifts to be discovered, developed and used to strengthen the church."[6]

A basic principle of the Protestant church is the "priesthood of believers." Even though many of our churches practice a two-tiered church structure, which we often label clergy and laity, it is not truly biblical. The Bible teaches that everyone who is saved has a ministry position in the church and has been gifted to fulfill it. Some are gifted to be pastors; others are gifted to be hospitable.

If you accept this value you will teach it to your students. You will let them know they need to be involved in ministry, and you will help them identify their ministry gift. Once a gift is identified, you will help your students develop it or connect with someone who can help.

We Build People Value Statement # 4

"Every believer has a purpose in advancing the global mission of Christ and the church."[7]

Teachers who accept this value statement recognize that the cycle of discipleship is not complete until the one being discipled has begun to disciple another. This discipleship can take place locally or globally. Often, those you disciple will reach even more people than you will. This multiplication principle of ministry reflects the desire of Jesus when He instructed all who would ever follow Him to "go and make disciples of all nations, baptizing them in the name of the Father and of the Son and of the Holy Spirit, and teaching them to obey everything I have commanded you. And surely I am with you always, to the very end of the age" (Matthew 28:19,20).

In the presentation of lessons, teachers must continually challenge their students to reach out to the lost and to fulfill the Great Commission of Jesus. All discipleship must point to this reproduction stage in the believer's life.

Expectations

Teachers who adopt a ministry philosophy and teach for its goals must expect that the results of their efforts will reflect that philosophy. Here are some ideas based on the *We Build People* ministry model.

Expect Spiritual Transformation

Each Sunday when you walk into the classroom, expect to make a difference in your students' lives. Through teaching God's Word, you become an essential part in their transformation. At the same time, the personal touch you add is also important to your students, whatever their ages.

Expecting spiritual transformation of students will take your attention off yourself and your performance, helping you focus on what is happening to the people in your classroom.

Expect the Holy Spirit to Be Present

If anything of eternal significance is going to happen to your students, the Holy Spirit's presence is essential in your classroom. So come to class prepared to teach the lesson. Note that being prepared includes the spiritual dimension: inviting the Holy Spirit into all aspects of the teaching/learning experience.

Help your students be open to the transforming power of the Holy Spirit. Always invite Him into the classroom as you begin to teach. Acknowledge His presence as He works through the interaction that takes place in the classroom.

Expect People to Develop Deeper Relationships With God

As a teacher, you can measure the progress of your students by their willingness to learn new things. Over time you should also be able to measure their progress by the transformation taking place in their lives. Students who are maturing spiritually will develop a desire to draw closer to God through the study of the Scriptures and through personal devotion.

Don't be satisfied with simply transmitting information from your notes to their notes. Don't measure your success simply by the number of memory verses your students can recite. Settle for nothing less than leading your students into a more meaningful relationship with their Savior. You will know this goal has been achieved when their attitudes become more Christlike and their deeds of service to God and people increase.

Expect Students to Take Part in the Classroom Ministry

A key element of spiritual maturity is exhibited when an individual takes responsibility for ministry. For example, as students mature in Christ, they should take on more of the ministry responsibilities of the classroom. Even young children can learn to hand out things; they can also learn to accept newcomers to their class—one of the most significant accomplishments of any age group. Such things are taught, and it's up to the teacher to teach them. Point out that assuming responsibilities in the classroom is to assume responsibilities within the body of Christ. It's often that practical. Therefore, willingness to accept such tasks or assignments is one measure of growth in a student's life.

Expect Numerical Growth

Numerical growth should not be the primary indicator of teaching success. But it is at least a secondary gauge. As students begin to draw closer to God and assume their proper roles in the classroom and the church, numerical growth will follow naturally. For example, people who fall in love with Jesus will naturally tell others about Him. As people are baptized in the Holy Spirit and receive the power to evangelize with boldness, they too will reach out. Once that happens, new converts will make their way into the church and probably into your classroom.

Expect a New Spiritual Dynamic

A teacher who helps students mature in their faith will find the teaching environment becoming spiritually charged. The Holy Spirit does His best work with believers who have hearts prepared to obey. Classrooms that were once boring will become exciting. Students who once looked at their watches anticipating dismissal will focus on the realm of the Spirit, anticipating His activity among them. People will come to class because they don't want to miss an encounter with the living God.

Evaluation

It is important that you are involved in an ongoing evaluation process of your ministry's success to students. Here are a few questions that will help you.

1. Are people outside the church being included?
2. Are people developing a deeper relationship with God?
3. Are people becoming involved in ministry?

Endnotes

[1]In 1999, the *We Build People* values were clarified and appear in this text as clarified. The original versions are cited here. Michael H. Clarensau, Sylvia Lee, Steven R. Mills, *We Build People, Making Disciples for the 21st Century,* (Springfield, Mo.: Gospel Publishing House, 1996), 11.

[2]Ibid., 11.

[3]Ibid., 25.

[4]Ibid., 25.

[5]Ibid., 31.

[6]Ibid., 35.

[7]Ibid., 38.

Teaching That Makes a Difference
Brings Creativity to the Classroom

By
Verda Rubottom

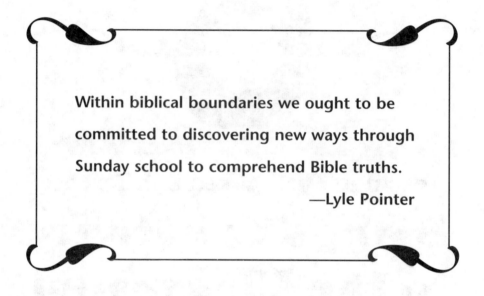

Within biblical boundaries we ought to be committed to discovering new ways through Sunday school to comprehend Bible truths.

—Lyle Pointer

The man seemed to appear out of nowhere. His robe was long, his face unshaven, and he had what could best be described as an "apostolic" appearance. He seated himself in the circle of teachers and began to describe the class he had been a part of almost two thousand years earlier. We will call it "the Class of '33."

"There were 12 of us, as I remember, in that very first class, and to say the least, we were a very unlikely group of students! My classmates by now have become household names in most of your churches. Their names were Peter, James, John, Matthew, Andrew, Philip, Nathanael, James the less, Judas Iscariot, Judas (brother of James), and Simon. It was quite a group and we were judged by many as the most unlikely group to become successful. However, for the most part, we did distinguish ourselves in later years.

"Our class facilities were relatively poor. In fact, you might even call them primitive. We had none of the equipment deemed necessary by modern standards. We had no campus, no buildings, no funds, no boards, no committees. However, we did have one thing that made all the difference. We had an incredible teacher! I believe we had *the* Teacher! He was the indispensable factor to our success. He was usually unassuming, yet always authoritative. He was practical, yet very idealistic. He respected tradition, yet did not seem bound by it. He honored the Law, yet He insisted that it be filled with life and love. His central theme was very simple: "If you want to know the truth, know me—*for I am truth!*" What is amazing is that there was not a single word of egotism in that statement. He was right! He personified Truth.

"When it came to the issue of teaching skills, He was a master. He made it a point to know us all intimately and individually. He would capture and hold our attention with knowledge that was both relevant and imaginatively presented. He illustrated profound concepts; He didn't get bogged down in detail. And He used variety to do it, which we appreciated. You know He was a good storyteller, but did you realize He used object lessons? There was the coin with Caesar's portrait, there was the little child that He set on His lap, and there was the temple itself! His visuals were ordinary enough—mustard seeds, millstones, birds, flowers in the fields—but they made His point. And when you saw them again, you remembered.

"He could certainly dramatize His points too. He changed water to wine in a matter of minutes, He fed five thousand with a few loaves and fish, and He raised Lazarus. And like I said, He personified His point at times: Besides being the Truth, He told us He was the Door, the Bread of Life, and the Good Shepherd. He could make demanding assignments, too, which taught us almost as much as the words He spoke. He even had us report on things, like what the people were saying about Him, who He was. And when He sent us out for field training, He wanted to know what happened.

"He almost always made His lessons apply to life, like when He told us not to rejoice as much about the spirits being subject to His name as much as about our names being written in heaven. That pulled us up short. He asked the hard questions and made some bold statements, which provoked discussion. When we asked questions, He would deal honestly with them. Even so, I have to admit we could be pretty slow. But He would explain himself, sometimes with a story, sometimes with the obvious question. Like

I said, our Teacher was a master in the art of communication.

"One of the many virtues that set him apart as Master Teacher was His genuine interest in the whole person. At the same time, He had some pretty high expectations, some sky-high standards, which He always explained. In fact, He was clear enough that some gave up following Him.

> On loyalty, He said, 'One God, that's it!'
> On motivation, He said, 'His kingdom first—seek it!'
> On commitment, He said, 'I want everything: heart and soul, mind and body!'
> On criticism, He said, 'And what about the log in your own eye?'
> On forgiveness, He said, 'Never stop forgiving!'
> On pride, He said, 'Come like a child.'
> On prayer, He said, 'Decide which you want, publicity or help, then pray accordingly.'
> On faith, He said, 'Just ask!'
> On heaven, He said, 'I'll have it ready when you get there!'

"Like I said, some turned back. But on the whole, this kind of teacher will get a following. All sorts of people came, probably all with different reasons. Some came hungering for bread; some came hungering for truth. Some came out of curiosity, just to see the miracles. But some came as spies—trying to get something on Jesus because His teaching threatened them. They wanted to find a way to break up what He'd started. Hard to believe, but before they were through they actually killed the Master Teacher and shut down His class...or so they thought! You can't bury the truth. They thought they could, but He refused to stay dead!

"I have to say that I was one of those who doubted His plan. Maybe that's because I was known as "The Doubter." My name is Thomas, and I'm from the Class of '33. But I can see now that His class is still open, that new students are enrolling every day. I can see that these teachers have learned their skills from the Master Teacher himself, just as we did. They are creative. Like us, they are

111

filled with His Spirit—and that makes them powerful. And just like Him, they can make a difference in individual lives."

Bringing creativity to the classroom sounds wonderful to some teachers but disconcerting to others. Clearly it can mean different things to different people. For some, allowing creative expression in a Sunday School class seems a little risky. They view creativity as a kind of free-for-all atmosphere, without guidance or structure. Others may believe that creative activities are a waste of time when there is so much serious learning that needs to take place.

These are legitimate concerns, especially in a class where things have gotten out of control. No one enjoys that kind of atmosphere, not even fun-loving children. Well-intended discussion groups in adult classes can start out focused, then veer onto tangents, leaving the teacher wondering whether valuable teaching time has been wasted. Creativity does not equal unstructured. Creativity need not be scary. Indeed, it can bring a level of delight to your classroom that you have never experienced before.

Reasons

A creative teacher is someone who goes beyond the routine and expected, someone who sparks the interest of students and makes Bible lessons come alive. We have all endured dull and monotonous teaching. At such a time, we tend to listen with our eyes, our minds wandering as the teacher plows steadily through the lesson material, oblivious to students' lack of interest. Some teachers have the false notion that the goal of the class session is to get through the lesson. But this is not how Sunday School should be. Our goal should be to teach so our students will have a greater hunger for the things of God and be transformed by the renewing of their minds (Romans 12:2).

Teaching at its best does not function as a one-way street. There should be an interchange of ideas between the student and the teacher. Opportunities for questions and answers should be included in every Sunday School lesson. Time should be allotted for activities that reinforce concepts and promote greater understanding. We need to challenge our students and encourage their participation in the learning process. How we do this will depend, of course, on the age and maturity of those we're teaching.

Responsibilities

Creativity in the classroom is composed of a variety of elements. Some of the more important elements will be discussed here.

God of Order and Creativity

Order and creativity are not incompatible. Creation clearly illustrates that God is a God of order—and creativity. His handiwork testifies to His creative power and order, as well as His majesty. David describes it beautifully: "The heavens declare the glory of God; the skies proclaim the work of his hands" (Psalm 19:1). But our Heavenly Father is concerned with the details of our lives as well as the big picture. Jesus said even the hairs of our head are all numbered (Matthew 10:30)!

We are comforted in knowing that God cares about us as individuals, that He is working out His plan through us. "'For I know the plans I have for you,' declares the Lord, 'plans to prosper you and not to harm you, plans to give you hope and a future'" (Jeremiah 29:11). This is the confidence every Sunday School teacher needs when stepping into the classroom each week. And this is one of the truths to convey to your students who have come to learn more about the character of our God.

God is with us as we do His work. We are not called to teach in

114

our strength alone. As teachers, we must be convinced that God wants us to succeed in the mission to which He has called us. Then we must lean on Him to work in and through us. With every assignment, God has promised to provide the strength and resources we need to accomplish the task. Philippians 4:19 assures us that God will supply all of our needs. First Thessalonians 5:24 encourages us with these words, "The one who calls you is faithful and he will do it." We need to remind ourselves of these promises frequently, because we are in a spiritual battle.

Obstacles to Creativity

Teachers are susceptible to discouragement and self-doubt. Even trained public school teachers become overwhelmed and leave the profession—in great numbers. Officials estimate that 40% of new teachers leave the profession within five years;[1] this, after years of study and a considerable financial investment.

Often church members decline to teach because they feel inadequate, particularly when it comes to teaching methods. They worry about keeping students' attention and presenting the lesson well. But this need not be an obstacle if we understand the value of creative teaching and are willing to learn new ways to teach.

When defining creativity you may think of such words as "imaginative," "original," "spontaneous," "talented," "inventive." While you may not think of yourself in any of those terms, we are all born with a measure of creativity. Unfortunately, life experiences can dampen it, causing us to doubt our abilities. Consequently, many adults describe themselves as "not very creative." Often, we compare ourselves with others and tend to limit creativity to the more obvious expressions of creative talent, as in art or music. Creativity, however, is not limited to these areas. For example, can you be flexible in your thinking? How are you at solving problems (you've heard of "creative" solutions)? Do you plan events with flair or enjoy new ideas?

Creative people can express their talents in many ways: through skillful hands, good ideas, novel solutions—and by the imaginative use of limited resources. A cardboard box can become a puppet stage, a church van can be transformed for a sidewalk Sunday School, and an open field can become a place for a community picnic, a neighborhood ball game, or a dirt bike track. Don't let resources determine your effectiveness. The limits we place on our resources hinder the possibilities. If Jesus could use a boy's lunch to feed thousands, God can multiply our resources as well.

Yet, as important as creativity is, we cannot rely on our talents alone for ultimate success in teaching. God expects us to develop and use our talents to their full potential but depend on His Spirit for the outcome.

What Is That in Your Hand?

When God spoke to Moses about leading the Israelites, He asked Moses a simple but significant question, "What is that in your hand?" (Exodus 4:2). Amazing, isn't it? The same rod Moses used to lead sheep in the desert would be used to lead God's people to freedom. God used a shepherd's rod in the hand of a faithful servant to demonstrate His miraculous power.

What do you have in your hand? What resources and abilities are you willing to make available for God's purposes? Take a moment now and offer God your time, your talent, and your resources. You may be surprised at what God will show you and how He will use the resources within your reach.

Preparation

We can identify creative people by how they think and the way they approach problems. They are open to new ideas and divergent, "out of the box" thinking. They understand there is usually more than one way to solve a problem, or present truth. We can see examples of this in Scripture.

In the Old Testament God spoke to His people in various ways: through a burning bush, on tablets of stone, through a whirlwind. He spoke through fearless prophets, through dreams and visions, and to a sleeping child. God did not limit himself to a single method of communicating with people. Neither should we.

Although Jesus used some of the customary teaching methods of the Jewish culture, on occasion He used unusual, even startling methods—cleansing the temple, walking on water, cursing a fig tree. His methods angered the religious leaders, who continually questioned His motives and authority. They were blinded by their extreme interpretation of the Law, which often lacked compassion and mercy. So Jesus had to go beyond the boundaries of their narrow thinking, sometimes literally; He went through Samaria, instead of around it, to reach a despised and rejected group of people. His methods of healing were equally astounding: using mud to heal blind eyes, actually touching lepers, and telling a crippled man to get up and carry his own bed! When necessary, Jesus crossed traditional boundaries to minister, to teach.

Other biblical examples also challenge us and cause us to reflect on the various ways God uses people to accomplish His will. Think of Moses, Gideon, and Nehemiah. All were chosen by God to accomplish great things, deeds beyond their natural ability. God delights in using ordinary people to accomplish extraordinary things. Expect God to do great things through you, just as He did in Bible days. This can happen as you spend time with God and allow the Holy Spirit to work through you as you teach. His touch will make all the difference.

We can prepare to teach with the expectation that God will use us in spite of any limitations of time and resources or lack of ability. We can rely on the Holy Spirit to guide us as we prayerfully make our plans. Here are some steps that will help you plan with purpose and creativity.

Preparing Your Lesson

When preparing to teach, take into consideration the age level, interests, and spiritual maturity of your students. People respond well to teachers who are familiar with their stage of life and have an understanding of the problems they face. They also respond to teachers who are enthusiastic about teaching and serving the Lord.

To be effective, a teacher will want to become familiar with new teaching methods for his or her age level in addition to currently used methods. For example, recent studies on learning styles and intelligences offer new insights on how people learn. Experts have identified eight different categories of intelligence and learning styles.[2] Further research may reveal more categories.

The eight intelligences (for which there are IQs) are linguistic, mathematical, spatial, musical, kinesthetic, intrapersonal, interpersonal, and naturalistic. These findings can help us plan lessons that include the learning styles of more of our students. Here are some clues to help you identify the learning styles.[3]

Linguistic—loves to read, write, tell stories; good speller, memorizes easily.

Mathematical—enjoys puzzles, computers; notices patterns; logical thinker.

Spatial—visualizes solutions; likes to draw, build, design, create; enjoys maps and charts; doesn't get lost.

Musical—remembers melodies; moves body to music; makes music.

Kinesthetic—mimics movements of others; athletic skill; handy with tools.

Intrapersonal—daydreams; works alone; identifies feelings.

Interpersonal—understands feelings of others; likes group projects, enjoys working with others; volunteers.

Naturalistic—knows names of stars and planets; enjoys bird-watching; sensitive to environment.

Some teachers may argue they just don't have the time to learn new teaching methods, learning styles, or age-level characteristics. But learning about new teaching methods need not be an overwhelming task. By simply using variety in your teaching, you will automatically engage more of the learning styles in your class.

One way to begin is simply to incorporate visuals and hands-on materials as much as possible. Children can participate in action songs and movement as they enjoy meaningful praise and worship songs. Small-group activities help those students who learn more easily through discussion and social interaction. Both large and small classes can benefit from using a variety of media. This can include everything from overheads to PowerPoint presentations to teaching videos. Object lessons, puppets, storytelling, balloon sculpture, and juggling are fun teaching tools for younger audiences. Don't feel that you have to be a performer to use these methods effectively. Simply start with what you have, and go from there. Be willing to try new methods, then choose what seems right for you and the age group you teach.

Remember your main responsibility as a Sunday School teacher: to help your students grow in their love for God and His Word and to teach them sound doctrine that will keep them on the right path (2 Timothy 4:1–3). Many methods for teaching and gaining the student's interest are available, but the best one is the one that works for you and your individual students. God will provide the tools and training you need to minister to the people He has called you to teach.

Developing a Creative Classroom

An essential principle that has influenced teachers over the years is "Interest precedes learning." The concept is basic, yet it demonstrates that to teach well, teachers need to think of ways to capture the interests of students.

Studies reveal that students respond to teachers who are positive, enthusiastic, and have high expectations of them.[4] These are key elements in a dynamic classroom. The teacher is responsible for creating an interesting, dynamic learning environment, a place where people, young and old alike, love to come for fellowship around God's Word.

In Sunday School, we are concerned with more than just information. Our goal should be to teach in a way that changes lives. Therefore, we must consider the needs of the whole person; that is, their physical, mental, emotional/social, and spiritual needs. For example, children who are hungry will have difficulty concentrating. Teenagers who are struggling with emotional issues may have no motivation to learn. Adults who come to Sunday School after a hard week may be exhausted. Feed the child. Pay attention to the teenager. Refresh the adult. The interest level of the people in your class will reflect how well you have planned to meet their needs. Teachers who realize the importance of meeting emotional and social needs will provide fellowship opportunities in class.

Such teachers are also aware that physical surroundings can enhance or detract from teaching. Everyone likes clean, orderly, and cheerful classrooms. As a teacher, it is worth coming a little early each week to make sure your classroom is in order for the arrival of your students. For example, children need space for movement and learning activities that direct their attention toward the lesson's Bible theme. Attention to these areas sends a positive message and will free you to make the best use of your limited teaching time.

The attentive teacher comes in at the right level for the students. This teacher is careful to plan lessons that are not too basic or redundant, but not above the students' heads either. Such are the challenges of developing a creative classroom.

Presentation

When you are planning your presentation, first look at the big picture. Know where you've been and where you want to take your students. Have an objective in mind that will help your students in their spiritual walk. Write down your objective and build your lesson around it. This should be the main truth you want your students to understand and remember. Ask God for direction and ideas on how to break down the spiritual principles you are teaching into easily digestible portions for your students. Finally, take time to evaluate student responses, including their overall participation.

Methods

Remember these things when you're looking for creative ways to present your material. Use appropriate methods for the age group you're teaching. Most children love spontaneity and participate readily in group activities. On the other hand, many adults hesitate about participating in a change of activity unless they are prepared for it. For example, some adults will volunteer a spontaneous testimony, but most will participate only if given time to organize their thoughts. Prepare your class for any change or special activity, especially in the case of teen and adult classes, since this will put them at ease and make them more likely to participate.

Remember: the younger the age, the more important it is to involve all the senses in the learning process. Visuals, of course, can be helpful at any age. Make sure they support and enhance your message rather than detract from it. People of any age can get caught up in a great presentation and—if it's not presented properly—forget the purpose behind it. Keep your message and your objective in focus at all times.

Teaching methods need not be complicated or expensive to be effective. Simple materials can illustrate great truths. Object lessons are a good example of how basic materials can drive home a truth that will be remembered for a long time.

In *Almost Everything I Need to Know About God I Learned in Sunday School*, Rob Parsons tells a story about a Sunday School teacher who made an indelible impression on his students.[5] The teacher asked the parents of his second grade students to help with next Sunday's lesson. Each student needed to bring a sack lunch from home instead of eating Sunday lunch with family.

Sunday morning the children arrived clutching their lunches and soon began asking when they could eat. Their requests were repeatedly denied. Fifteen minutes before the end of class, the teacher asked, "Now, what if I asked you to give your lunch away?" The children gasped. He had their attention. So after giving them permission to eat, he told them the story of Jesus feeding the five thousand. Now the children could identify with a boy in Bible days who offered his lunch to help feed the crowd. This true story illustrates how a creative teacher brought a Bible story to life in the hearts of young children.

A classic object lesson shows the importance of getting along with other people. The only materials needed are seven sticks and some string or rope.

A farmer had seven sons. He was proud of all of his boys, and he looked forward to watching them grow into manhood. One of the things he looked forward to the most was watching them grow in their relationships with each other. *Someday when I am old,* he thought, *I will still be happy because my sons and their families will have each other.* He imagined they would always be friends and be there to help each other. But as the boys grew older, the farmer became sad. Despite all his blessings, there was one thing he didn't have. He had a loving wife, the mother of his seven sons, and a prosperous farm. But the thing that made him sad was his boys—they were always fighting each other. When they got up in the morning they began to fight, and it continued throughout the day. It seemed there was always strife and unhappiness among them. His dream of his sons growing up to be friends was fading because they could not get along.

Then one day he got an idea. He told the boys that he had something important to talk to them about. One by one he called them in, the youngest to the oldest. On the table he had a bundle of sticks tied with a cord. He said to the youngest

122

son, "If you can break these sticks, I'll give you one of the colts that will be born this spring." Then he let the boy try. But try as he might, the boy could not break the bundle of sticks. The farmer called the next oldest son and he tried as well. The farmer called in each one of his sons and offered them the same prize if they could break the bundle of sticks. But even the strongest of the seven boys could not break them. *(If you're teaching children, allow them to try to break the bundle of sticks you've tied together.)*

Finally, he called them all in together. He told them of his broken heart, how sad he was that the sons he loved had not become friends. He said, "Sons, not one of you could break these sticks, and I'll tell you why. These sticks—all seven of them—are tied together. You see, when the sticks are held together by this cord, which represents love and friendship, they become too strong to be broken. In the same way, a family that is bound together cannot be broken. No enemy is strong enough to hurt it. But there is a way to break the sticks, and that is by separating them. Then, one by one, they can be broken. It's easy that way. *(Demonstrate breaking the sticks one by one.)* So, you see, my sons, when you don't hold together, an enemy can come in and, by separating us, break us one by one and destroy the family. But when we stick together, we are too strong for our enemies."[6]

The sons realized what their broken-hearted father was trying to tell them. And from that day on they decided to stick together, through the good and the bad times. They loved and forgave each other. They became friends again. Just so, God wants our families to be strong, our churches to be strong, and our friendships to be strong. We can have this bond when we stick together.

This is an example of a simple object lesson that illustrates a great truth. It is also one that most age groups can understand and relate to.

You can also gain the interest of your class by utilizing the latest technological media and the gifts of people who are skilled in them. What once took hours to prepare can now be prepared in minutes. Become familiar with the capabilities of computers and the various forms of media technology. Don't overlook the creative new art materials available at art and hobby stores.

Organization

As stated earlier, creativity and organization are compatible and necessary. You will especially need good organization and planning when using creative materials with young children. Setting down guidelines before a learning activity and having all your materials ready will cut down on confusion and noise levels. Have other teachers help you organize the activities and assign their specific responsibilities ahead of time.

Elementary children should be involved in set-up and clean-up activities. Children learn by having responsibilities and should not have everything done for them. Elementary children thrive on participation. They gain confidence when they are given opportunities to learn by helping.

Don't limit the use of class assistants or team teaching only to younger grade levels. Youth and adult classes benefit from people with organizational and technical skills, as well as those who have the gift of hospitality. Using people who are willing to contribute their skills will increase the participation and interest level of your class. You are also helping people grow in their gifts when you give them opportunities to use their skills.

Being organized allows for flexibility. Creative teachers are flexible. They look for "teachable moments" and special opportunities. They know when it's time to stop teaching to pray for a special need or take advantage of a life-related question. Creative teachers are not so locked into a schedule that they miss some of the most rewarding aspects of teaching, such as getting to know their students individually, taking time to explain important concepts, or sharing what God has done for them personally. Be flexible within the structure you have planned, and always leave room for the Holy Spirit to redirect your plans.

Expectations

What can you expect from your efforts to bring creativity to the classroom? For one thing, your students will want to come to class each week. They will have their minds stretched, their spirits strengthened, and their roots buried a little deeper into the Word. How refreshing to have a teacher who can't wait to get to Sunday School to share from the heart and teach in a way that is exciting, creative, and relevant!

Your students will respond to your enthusiasm about teaching. Children will share show-and-tell treasures with their teacher, teens will linger after class with good news, adults will feel more comfortable requesting prayer for a family need. Teaching will be even more fulfilling as you begin to move beyond the duties expected to the creative possibilities God has in store for you as a teacher.

Evaluation

1. What challenges do you face with your attempts to be creative in the classroom?
2. What help did you receive on creativity in this chapter?
3. How does understanding the various types of learners help in your quest for creativity?
4. What methods do you regularly use in your teaching, and what methods do you wish to try in the future?
5. To whom can you go for help in developing your creative skills?

Endnotes

[1]Harry K. and Rosemary Tripi Wong, *The First Days of School: How To Be an Effective Teacher* (Sunnyvale, Calif.: Harry K. Wong Publications, 1991), v.

[2]D.R. Cruickshank, D.L. Bainer, K.K. Metcalf, *The Act of Teaching* (St. Louis, Mo.: McGraw Hill, 1999), 323.

[3]*Guideposts for Kids* (May/June 2001), 6–8.

[4]Cruickshank, Bainer, Metcalf, *The Act of Teaching,* 42.

[5]Rob Parsons, *Almost Everything I Need to Know About God I Learned in Sunday School* (Nashville, Tenn.: Thomas Nelson, 1999), 66–7.

Teaching That Makes a Difference
Connects Beliefs to Behavior

By
Carey Huffman

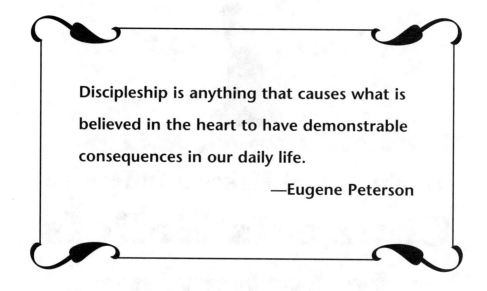

Discipleship is anything that causes what is believed in the heart to have demonstrable consequences in our daily life.

—Eugene Peterson

How could this be happening? Perhaps the mental taxation of three years of college life and the impending mid-term exams were taking their toll, filling every recess of his mind and hindering even the slightest recollection. But his memory had always served him well in the past. True, his mind seemed to have more affinity for recalling concepts and facts, information and details, than for remembering the personal, sentimental aspects of life. But he was preparing for full-time ministry, and it seemed that concern for people should be making more of an impression on his thinking.

Besides, this situation was different. There was no excuse for it. She had been a friend for almost a year. It had taken him most of that time just to muster the nerve to ask her out. So it wasn't as if memories of other relationships were clouding his mind. If her birthday, or even the occasion of their second date, had slipped his mind, that would have been understandable, forgivable. But this was much more serious, and it was about to spell the end of a long-anticipated relationship. After just one night out, he had done the unimaginable—he had forgotten what she looked like.

True, he would have recognized her when she came to her door (he did remember where she lived). At the moment, however, her image had escaped his mind. Memories of other aspects of her personality and interests—that she played the piano, taught Sunday School, and loved pizza—were still intact, but he couldn't connect them to anything physical. Then again, he did know that she had long, dark hair—and for a moment it seemed as if he could even hear her voice—but he just couldn't put a face with it. Was this weird or what? As he lay there on the top bunk, staring at the ceiling, he reverted to one of his childhood pastimes of trying to make out a profile, her profile, in the cracks and crevices of the tile above—nothing.

Then, a glimmer of hope arose from an unlikely object. It was nothing in the room. It was in his mind. It was something about her appearance that he could recall. Perhaps he would recover from his memory lapse in time for their second date after all, thanks to those bold, almost gaudy, earrings she wore most of the time. They would turn out to be the beacon that would lead him out of this mental haze. For some odd reason, the big turquoise triangles dangled in his mind. From there he could vaguely picture the ears they were attached to, then the hair, the eyes, the face; before long, the image was complete. The date was still on.

However, this embarrassing sequence of events likely accounts for the fact that the second date was the last. To be certain, they had a nice enough time that night (understandably, she was never made aware of her date's missing memory), and the breakup was never really formalized. It just seemed appropriate not to pursue the relationship. His forgetfulness made it obvious that he had put limited stock in the relationship, that it meant very little to him.

James 1:23,24 says that "anyone who listens to the Word but does not do what it says is like a man who looks at his face in a mirror and, after looking at himself, goes away and immediately forgets what he looks like."

We all forget a face from time to time, but usually not our own; that would be absurd. Yet, this is what happens with God's Word, if after being exposed to it, we never put it into practice. The Word gives us a very stark glimpse of ourselves, our tendencies, shortfalls, motives, even our potential in Christ. But if we walk away from the mirror of Scripture and do not act on it, the truth is as good as forgotten. It will make absolutely no difference in our lives, other than to callous our minds to the transforming and renewing power of God's Word in the future.

"But the man who looks intently into the perfect law that gives freedom, and continues to do this, not forgetting what he has heard, but doing it—he will be blessed in what he does" (James 1:25).

Why aren't the nearly one hundred million church members in America having a greater effect on the moral and spiritual climate of our society?

If there were a "top ten" list of reasons why people reject faith in Christ, the following excuse would probably be number one: It goes like this: "Well I know this person who is supposed to be a Christian and she...Christians are hypocrites!" An all-too-common objection to the faith is not the claims of Christ but the conduct of His people—those who profess to be Christian but aren't living a life to back it up. People at large are rejecting Christ because they are not seeing Him in the people who claim His Name.

Do we need a more powerful case for raising the standard of authentic Christian conduct, for challenging and equipping our students to practice what they profess, to connect their beliefs to behavior?

Reasons

My four-year-old daughter loves to quote Scripture. But reciting "I can do all things..." is one thing, actually facing the dark is another. She'll even remind herself "Children obey your parents..." as she proceeds to ignore my instruction. Perhaps such behavior is understandable with little children. But a similar detachment of faith from experience is filtering through society. Many people today, even in the church, see no problem when their principles do not line up with their practice and spiritual decisions don't affect specific demonstration. A person may have beliefs, but no real faith.

Instead of Christianity being a way of life, it becomes only one slice of the pie of life. With Jesus confined to His portion, the other areas of life remain untouched by Him. Ron Hutchcraft refers to this as "compartmentalized Christianity": the modern way to follow Jesus. People visit their "Jesus slice" at church regularly—sing the songs, feel the feelings, review the beliefs—then go out to live as they please in the other slices of life.[1] As a teacher, you must strive to connect learning to life, challenging and equipping students with a Christianity that flavors every part of their lives. If Bible truth never makes it past the head, into the heart, and ultimately out "through the hand," certain consequences will inevitably follow.

The Cold, Hard Facts

Spiritual complacency, even outright insensitivity to God's Word, inevitably results from scriptural knowledge that is left unapplied. A lack of spiritual appetite is usually a by-product of a weak, unexercised faith.

Truth Isn't Learned Until It's Lived

Even the deepest spiritual understanding will never transform a life. Real growth occurs only when Bible knowledge is applied to real life. Medical students can have a wealth of textbook knowledge without being ready to perform surgery. Student pilots may have mastered the flight simulator, but that doesn't mean they're ready to take a planeload of passengers cross-country. James 1:22 says, "Do not merely listen to the Word, and so deceive yourselves. Do what it says." People are not to be merely informed by the Word; they are to be transformed by the Word. It could be argued that a person truly believes only the part of the Bible that they actually do.

133

Faith Is Affirmed by Action

Faith is not a passive notion, not a spectator sport. It is meant to be active and vibrant. When accumulating biblical knowledge is mistaken for spiritual growth, it becomes much easier to continue without the intention of bringing the Word to life. People become accustomed to powerless faith, their hearts hardened to the point where life-changing truth never breaks into reality. James reminds us that "faith by itself, if it is not accompanied by action, is dead" (James 2:17). Answering the self-congratulatory person who acts as if belief in God is enough, James points out that "even the demons believe that." He then supplies "evidence that faith without deeds is useless"(2:19,20) by citing Abraham and Rahab. At opposite ends on the scale of worthies, they were nevertheless equals in this matter of "faith and...actions...working together" (2:22). If people never apply their faith in real-life situations, they never grow in their relationship with Christ. Why should God reveal more of himself to those who are doing little with what they already know?

Spiritual Deficiencies

An anemic faith, lacking spiritual stamina and resistance, is symptomatic of, and susceptible to, a number of other serious spiritual maladies that affect the individual, the church, and the world.

Limited "Lordship"

Jesus asked the question: "Why do you call me 'Lord, Lord' and do not do what I say?" (Luke 6:46). Our relationship with Jesus cannot be limited to a few aspects of life—it must include every aspect—that's true Lordship.

Missing Parts

When individuals don't apply their faith to spiritual maturity, the body of Christ is left malnourished, underdeveloped. Entire congregations suffer as a result, occupied with spiritual infants of all ages. The apostle Paul challenges us to "become mature, attaining to the whole measure of the fullness of Christ. Then we will no longer be infants, tossed back and forth by the waves, and blown here and there by every wind of teaching" (Ephesians 4:13,14).

Distorted Views

The world is taking note of those who profess faith in Christ, for good or for bad, and its perception of God himself is often based on what it sees. When a Christian's behavior is inconsistent with professed "beliefs," the world gets a blurred image of Christ. Consequently, people who do not have a personal relationship with Him are left with one of two reactions. They will either reject the Christian faith because of what they see as hypocrisy, or worse, accept the distortion as an accurate and acceptable representation. The real Jesus is never seen; His true story is never told.

Responsibilities

Our Great Commission is not to make "believers"; it is to make disciples. A disciple is a "learner and follower." Once again, people don't really learn Christ's ways until they actually follow them. A common misperception in the American church is that you can be a Christian but not a disciple. People may come to church, participate in programs, and give money but, in reality, they lack a personal commitment to Christ. Church leaders carry the burden of trying to motivate these people to do what they don't want to do. In an interview for *Cutting Edge* newsletter, Dallas Willard states, "We must teach people to think clearly about what a disciple really is—a person who has decided that the most important thing in their life is to learn how to do what Jesus said to do. A disciple is not a person who has things under control, or knows a lot of things. Disciples simply are people who are constantly revising their affairs to carry through on their decision to follow Jesus."[2]

An indispensable aspect of the discipleship process is evident in Jesus' command: "Go...make disciples....*teaching* them to obey" (Matthew 28:19,20, emphasis mine). The result of practical, biblical instruction should be more thoroughly-equipped disciples.

Lay a Foundation for Disciple-making

Teaching does not automatically produce disciples, and yet, the making of disciples is not possible without a broad base of consistent, practical teaching in the Word. Acts 1:1 refers to "all that Jesus began to do and to teach." In other words, we are to continue what Jesus began. As disciple-makers, teachers must follow the example laid out by Jesus, the ultimate disciple-maker. In addition to His reliance on the Father for guidance and the Holy Spirit for power, Jesus' ministry was marked by these requirements of effective discipleship:

Relationship

He called them that they might be with Him (Mark 3:13,14). We must never sidestep the personal, individual nature of making disciples. Relationship must be at the heart of all you do with students if you are to shape their lives spiritually.

Relevance

He spoke in their terms (common language and parables) and to their needs. Regardless of the importance of the message, people are not likely to pay attention unless they can see a connection to their lives and concerns.

Reason

Jesus demonstrated the ultimate purpose for living: to love God, to reflect His love toward others, and to spread the message of forgiveness and eternal life in Him (John 15:12–17). Likewise, give students a vision, and the discipline to accomplish it will often follow.

Release

He sent them out with the opportunity and authority to exercise their faith and giftings, even though they did not yet understand everything (Luke 9:2; 10:1–19). For many people today, practical experience substantiates truth. Boredom and apathy set in if faith is not exercised and ministry outlets are not provided.[3]

Since effective teaching is essential for true discipleship, your ministry in and out of the classroom must be characterized by the foregoing elements of relationship, relevance, reason, and release. The goal of your class, as a vital part of the discipleship process, should be to encourage and empower students to live what they learn, and to be who God created them to be.

Set an Example

People learn far more from what they see and do than from what they hear, study, or simply think about. When a teacher can say as the apostle Paul, "Follow my example, as I follow the example of Christ" (1 Corinthians 11:1), that teacher is laying out a pattern for discipleship. When teachers do not practice what they profess, their teaching lacks credibility and authenticity. How you embrace and enact the truth yourself will determine what you can expect of students. Although you are with the students on a limited basis, never underestimate the ability of your character and conduct to either confirm or deny what you present in class.

Equip Them to Serve

Take comfort; you don't have to do everything. Ministry leaders are not fulfilling their biblical mandate until they "prepare God's people for works of service" (Ephesians 4:12) and eventually turn parts of their own ministry over to others. This requires a plan to instill ministry values, a continuing challenge to students to find a place of involvement, and a provision of opportunities for ministry within the class setting and beyond.

Give Them Something to Do

We live in an experience-driven culture. For many people, experience validates knowledge. They believe and accept what they can personally experience: "try it before you buy it." Although "experience" is not always feasible, we can take advantage of the fact that activity creates a context for learning. Young children learn by doing, and elementary kids thrive on acquiring new skills and abilities. Young teens need a sense of achievement, while high school and college students often gain a sense of purpose through broader community involvement. Most adults want their participation in anything to make a real-life difference in family life. Students of all ages want their lives to hold significance.

Teach Them to Share Their Faith

The reason many Christians are apprehensive about sharing their faith is not unbelief, fear of rejection, or shame. Quite simply, they are not sure what to say or how to respond when witnessing opportunities arise. As teachers, we can equip students with tools that inspire confidence in handling—even pursuing—such opportunities. Obviously students don't need to master an evangelism course in order to communicate the Gospel, but this subject merits much more attention than we often give it. Students at all levels need biblical training that equips them to share absolutes in a morally and spiritually pluralistic society.

Preparation

Even the most significant purpose crumbles without a solid plan. It's not enough just to know where you want to go. You must

138

determine your direction and destination before you prepare the lesson. In this respect, teaching is much like planning a trip. Your destination—students doing something with what they learn—must guide your entire approach to the lesson so that students are challenged and equipped to apply truth to life in very specific and practical ways.

A Travel Plan

Where Are You Going?

Start with the end in mind. Each lesson should have a specific and stated objective, an overriding theme or purpose. Every lesson point, activity, discussion, and ministry should develop the theme and point to specific actions. If you intend for students to do something practical with the instruction they receive, your lesson must be aimed at showing them what and how.

How Will You Get There?

Plot your course. Start with the familiar, relating the truth to current and common situations, and develop the theme from there. Be prepared to cross the obstacles and bridges—questions and difficulties that must be addressed—in order for students to accept the truth as well as to act on it.

Are You Packed Accordingly?

Have you ever started a trip with the thought, "What am I forgetting?" or arrived, only to realize that you left something essential behind? Think through each element of the lesson and be sure you have what you need to introduce the lesson, illustrate main points, involve students, and enhance retention.

What Will You Do Along the Way?

Where will you stop? What sights will you see? What are you likely to talk about? Plan activities that will enrich the journey and make it more memorable. To keep it interesting, break up the time, but stay on track and keep moving in a timely fashion toward your destination.

An Action Plan

What Will You Do Once You Get There?

Classes often get so preoccupied with the journey that they never reach their destination. Even if they do arrive, they have no time to carry out their original plans. Arrive "in time" to do what you came to do and see what you came to see. You took a specific route to a specific destination in order to do certain things. At all costs, reserve enough time for discussion, planning, or a practical exercise that demonstrates the difference the truth should make in real life. Just as vacations are a time to relax, a journey through the Word should bring refreshment and relief from the hassles of life. Unless you come away with a renewed readiness to face the work-a-day world, the trip didn't serve its ultimate purpose.

Don't Forget the Souvenirs.

When children bring handwork home from class, it's more than decoration for the refrigerator. It is a concrete expression of what was learned. The same principle applies to all ages. Just as pictures and memorabilia serve as reminders of good times, you can reinforce the message beyond class time by giving students something to take away from the session. This may be a tangible item, a practical exercise, a very memorable illustration, or a particularly relevant action step. A large part of bringing lessons to life is keeping students mindful of the challenge long enough for them to start living it.

Presentation

A teacher cannot completely affect what students do—in class or out. Even when it appears that truths are learned and decisions made, many never follow through on their good intentions. However, an effective teacher will consistently do several things to ensure that students can correlate truth to life. If your class sessions are going to make a practical difference in your students' lives by helping them connect their beliefs to behavior, the following directives must characterize your lessons.

Make Lessons Relevant

Regardless of a message's importance, most people will pay little attention to it unless they can see what it has to do with their lives and concerns "right here, right now." Very practical and obvious connections should be drawn from the lesson to everyday life. Be a student of your students, alert to their needs and aware of what's going on in their lives. You will hold their attention and provoke greater response as you make increasing effort to relate to your students.

Make Lessons Challenging

By dealing with tough issues, questions, and concerns already on your students' minds, you help them see the relevance of their faith to real life. Other people and situations in life will challenge their faith. As a friend, you should help them challenge it first. An unchallenged faith is not owned.

Make Lessons Memorable

Creativity is one of the most valuable assets a teacher can develop, but creativity is not an end in itself. It serves the greater purpose of making a unique and lasting impression. Be prepared—if you frequently use a lot of vivid and lively illustrations, some church members may accuse you of peddling a frivolous message, a message without spiritual depth. In this case, you may want to graciously ask the skeptics to recount for you two or three sermons they have heard lately. Chances are, they will be able to recall only a few sketchy and assorted points. On the other hand, many of your students will probably be able to rattle off the theme of several past messages because of the illustrations you've used. The point is this: No matter how capable the communicator, if people forget the message right away, it does them no good. If students don't remember the message long enough to put it into practice, then it will never make a difference in their lives.

Make your lessons more memorable by incorporating some of these methods: video or audio clips, a tie to current issues and events, a unique drama or anecdote, personal testimonies, active illustrations, humorous activities, music and visuals, unpredictable object lessons, spontaneous melodrama, and use of media and technology. Using such methods throughout a lesson provides variety, promotes interest, and provokes student response in and out of class.

Make Lessons Interactive

If you want students to act on the truth later, then let them act on it now. Get students involved; engage as many senses as possible throughout the lesson. Use a variety of discussion starters, including agree/disagree, role-playing, and case-study scenarios. Interject personal testimonies or use drama to depict real-life experiences. Interactive illustrations and application exercises that reinforce main points can engage students using a variety of means, spoken and written. Providing outlines and response sheets can help students retain much more, even if they never refer to the notes again. Finally, consider having students assist with teaching. This will allow you direct discipleship opportunities as you help them prepare for their part. Remember, effective discipleship includes not only ministry *to* students, but more importantly, *with* students and *by* students. When people are actively involved in the learning process, they gain interest and retain more.

Make Lessons Specific and Practical

Too often we speak in vague spiritual terms about God—what He is saying or what He wants us to do—instead of using concrete, specific terms. By determining with each lesson exactly what you want students to grasp about following Christ, you can lead them into situations that will give them a real-life taste of that truth. Help students determine specific ways that truth translates to life in school, at home, on the job. Get students in the habit of asking Jesus, "What do you want to do in my life today?"

Make Lessons Purposeful

If students are going to act on what they are learning in class, they must see a reason for it. An athlete would not continue to endure drills and practices if there was no contest in which to participate. All Christians are called into the action. However, leaders often wait so long to put their people in the game that by the time they're called onto the field, they have already joined the spectators in the stands. Some have left the stadium altogether. Practical involvement and real responsibility that make an obvious difference in their lives or the lives of others is appealing to most people. When they appear unmotivated, it is often due to a lack of vision. When students grasp a vision and purpose, motivation and discipline will follow.

Make Lessons Inclusive of Personal Ministry

Christian education must include personal, practical ministry. If we want signs to accompany ministry of the Word, time must be given in class for Spirit-led, Spirit-dependant ministry. One of the most important lessons we can teach students is how to pray. The best way for them to learn is to actually do it. We often spend far more time sharing concerns than praying for them. Occasionally dividing into pairs or small groups will allow more time for individuals to share needs and receive prayer. Another novel way to cover requests is to have students pray their concerns to God while the rest of the group agrees with them. Before class is over, be sure to take time to pray for issues directly related to the lesson topic and its life application.

Make Lessons Accountable

It's difficult to keep up with every student's spiritual progress. Take time at the outset of class sessions for brief testimonies and feedback from students about their experiences in applying truths of previous lessons. Besides giving you a general impression of the class's progress, you extend the life of previous lesson challenges. Students may be more inspired to actually do what they intend to do if they expect to be accountable to any degree.

Make Lessons a Matter of Principle

If students' spiritual knowledge and beliefs are going to shape their behavior, they must learn to govern their lives by principles. Principles are predetermined guidelines or standards built on clear convictions. With principles, decisions about attitudes and behaviors are made once. When an issue or temptation arises, the decision has already been made. The issue is not reconsidered on the spur of the moment or in the heat of passion. A person who must labor over the same decision each time it arises has not settled on a principle for guidance and, therefore, is more likely to fall by a reckless and destructive decision—remember Samson.

Make Lessons a Matter of Passion

When Jesus asked Peter repeatedly, "Do you love me?" (John 21:15–17), He was trying to establish a priority in Peter's life. It is still the primary question to be answered by true disciples today. Spiritual power and sensitivity flow from a love relationship with Christ. After Jesus' arrest, the disciples scattered because of the threat of the Sanhedrin. After the resurrection and the coming of the Holy Spirit, it was a different story. With power and passion, the disciples now made an able reply before the Sanhedrin, and its members recognized that the disciples "had been with Jesus" (Acts 4:13). Trying to serve God or "live right" out of a sense of obligation will not work; commitments stemming from such motivation will usually be short-lived. God wants us to serve Him from a heart of gratitude, responding to His love by loving Him in return, because we are now free to do the things we should. We would not choose to do otherwise because we have a relationship that means more to us than anything else; we would not want to compromise it for any other gain. Teach students to live and serve out of love for Jesus; then their life's priorities and practices will align with His plans and purposes.

Expectations

Our purpose in teaching, as a means of discipleship, is to help students translate their faith into action—beliefs to behavior—both in and out of the church. Where lessons end, living the truth should begin. By the conclusion of any session, your students should be able to answer the question, "What do I need to do now that I know this?" As an effective teacher committed to enacting the principles that lead students to live what they are learning, you can expect to help individual class members do the following:

Foster Their Maturity

The goal of every Sunday School class, small group, and discipleship ministry should be to produce maturity in the lives of its members. Accomplishing that goal requires giving students not only things to know, but things to be and to do, because the purpose of God's Word in our lives is two-fold: change in character (who I am) and change in conduct (what I do). The evidence of growth and change should become more apparent as our focus turns from what we get out of ministry to how we can contribute. A mature individual who is determined to act upon knowledge of the Word will commit to serving God by serving others—no matter what is received in return.

Find Their Ministry

The sign of a healthy ministry, church, or Sunday School class is one that helps all its members identify their gifts and express them through serving in ministry. Your role as a teacher is imperative, since your gift and calling is to help others discover, develop, and deploy their gifts to the church: "to prepare God's people for works of service, so that the body of Christ may be built up" (Ephesians 4:11,12).

My preschool-age daughter loves to open Christmas presents—hers and everyone else's. While I'm trying to teach her to be unselfish, her eagerness challenges me in this way: We should never outgrow the childlike desire to help each other open the gifts God has given us. So many gifts to the body of Christ sit on the shelf unnoticed, unopened, unused—recipients either unaware of their gifts or reluctant to open them in front of anyone. Don't let your students be "unopened gifts." Your class should be a safe place for students to reveal and receive God-given gifts. Pastor Rick Warren suggests using the S.H.A.P.E. model to help people discover their place of greatest effectiveness.

146

Spiritual Gift

What natural-born abilities and talents do you possess? People are fulfilled when they serve in their area of gifting.

Heart

What is your passion? What do you love to do? High achievers are most often those who enjoy what they do.

Abilities

What do you do well? There are many specific talents and potential ministries not identified in the "spiritual gift" passages (Romans 8; 1 Corinthians 12; Ephesians 4)—for example, musical talent, art, research—that can be put to use in any number of creative ways. "It seems better," writes Dr. Stanley Horton, "to take all of these lists as merely giving samplings of the gifts and callings of the Spirit, samplings taken from an infinite supply."[4]

Personality

How will your uniqueness affect your service? Be content with what God has placed in you and develop it. When people serve in a manner consistent with their God-given personality, they experience fulfillment, satisfaction, and fruitfulness.

Experiences

How can your experiences (skills or circumstances), good and bad, be used to help others? God never wastes experiences, including misguided and painful ones.[5]

No student should sit long in your class wondering what his or her gifts, abilities, and successes are. Your job is to point out and affirm strengths to your students, and to others. As needed, spend time with individual students exploring avenues of service (some of which your class can provide) and steer them into the practical training opportunities and service outlets available in your church. Once they know, and have direction for, their gifts, the question changes from "How do I grow?" to "Where do I serve?"

By providing opportunities for students to serve, you are helping them become comfortable using their gifts. Look at the students God has placed in your trust and develop your ministry around them; find unique and significant ways for each of them to serve according to his or her level of maturity and desire.

Fulfill Their Mandate

The purpose of a disciple is to know Jesus and to make Him known: to grow in godliness and Christlike behavior and to go in loving obedience to spread the Good News. Neither of these will be fulfilled without the solid instruction and practical application of God's Word. The Pharisees knew the Word inside and out and yet, the spirit of the Law never made its way into their hardened hearts, let alone out through their hypocritical lives. They refused to be like the proverbial wise man, which Jesus says "hears these words of mine and puts them into practice." Is your class full of apathetic believers or active disciples? The world will recognize Jesus for who He really is only as true believers reflect the actions demonstrated and directed by the Word. It has never been easy to live for Christ, but Christ is life. We must challenge our students to communicate and demonstrate that life to empty, hurting, and searching people. More than something to believe in, they need Someone to live for.

Evaluation

The following questions will help you as a teacher gauge and improve your ability to help students connect their beliefs to their behavior.